Love's Orphan

My Journey of Hope and Faith

Ildiko Scott

Love's Orphan

My Journey of Hope and Faith

Ildiko Scott

Alive Book Publishing

Dedication

This book is dedicated to my father
whose strong will, perseverance and love of America
set the path for me to follow in his footsteps.

For all these qualities, I am forever grateful.

Thank you
Ildiko

Love's Orphan: My Journey of Hope and Faith
Copyright © 2016 by Ildiko Scott

Additional copies may be ordered from the publisher for
educational, business, promotional or premium use.
For information, contact ALIVE Book Publishing at:
alivebookpublishing.com, or call (925) 837-7303.

Book Design by Alex Johnson

ISBN 13
978-1-63132-026-2

ISBN 10
16313202642

Library of Congress Control Number: 2016930463

Library of Congress Cataloging-in-Publication Data
is available upon request.

First Edition

Published in the United States of America by
ALIVE Book Publishing and ALIVE Publishing Group,
imprints of Advanced Publishing LLC
3200 A Danville Blvd., Suite 204, Alamo, California 94507
alivebookpublishing.com

PRINTED IN THE UNITED STATES OF AMERICA

10 9 8 7 6 5 4 3 2 1

Contents

Foreword

One early spring evening, I was driving home from work just as the sun was setting behind Mount Diablo in northern California. The sky was coral-red with contrasting puffy gray clouds, and the hills were vivid green and smelling fresh from the winter rains. I couldn't help but say a simple prayer of thanks to God for all this beauty around me. As I drove into our beautiful and peaceful neighborhood I gave thanks, as I always do, for my many blessings, for my wonderful husband, for our amazing children, for our many special friends, and for all the opportunities I have been given in this great country called the United Sates of America.

How did I get here? Where did the master plan for my life come from? I do believe there is a plan for everyone's life and that we follow the path set out for us. While I know all this I am still in awe of the fact that I am here and in America against all odds. Though I know I will never lose my Hungarian roots, I also know that the day I became an American citizen in 1971—when I pledged allegiance to the flag of this country—America became my homeland. It was a long road, but it has been worth it every step of the way.

I have often wondered if I should write about my long journey from Hungary to America. I would think, *Who wants to read another life story? Doesn't everyone have a story to tell?* Though I resisted for many years writing about my life, the supportive prompting of many of my acquaintances, my friends, and most important my husband and children, helped me decide to write my story.

Though some of this now seems so long ago, from another time and place, I still believe it is a story that will inspire people. It is a story of survival and hope. It is a story of overcoming rejection, pain, and loneliness as a child. It is a story about finding faith in God.

It is my hope that as you read this book you will find that you can also change your destiny in spite of the current circumstances you find yourself in. You can let go of the pain and forgive everyone who hurt you. You can be free to become the person God intends you to be.

I would like to thank my husband, Jud, who encouraged me for so many years to write my story. I also would like to thank our son, Nathan, and our daughter, Lauren, because they convinced me that my story would be a legacy they could pass on to their children. After all, this is their story too!

Prologue

We visited Hungary, the country of my birth, with our children the summer before my mother got sick. Nathan was six and Lauren was almost three. The first thing I wanted to do was return to the orphanage to have a picture taken at the back of the courtyard where I would sit by the iron fence and dream of freedom. Where I would look outside and wonder what life would be like if I ever got out of there.

I spent some of the loneliest times of my life at this orphanage, and my "special" spot by the fence had taken on deep significance in my memory and heart. I would sit there hoping, nearly always in vain, that my mother would come see me. I would watch families walking by, parents holding the hands of their children, laughing, smiling, and loving each other with such natural ease. *Wow, I* thought; *what is that like?*

And there I was once more, this time with my loving husband, Jud, and our beautiful family. Never in my wildest dreams could I have imagined the turns my life would take, and that it would bring me so far from these humble, and often very sad, beginnings.

Being born in 1947, I arrived in the middle of a very tragic and difficult century for Hungary, and my childhood and early teen years seem now a mirror for the struggles of our people during that era. My life then, as with my former country, was trapped amid opposing forces and torn between conflicting ideologies against a backdrop of debilitating loss.

World War I had been devastating to Hungary, which had entered the conflict as part of the sturdy Austro-Hungarian Empire. Its wealth gone, economy ruined, and regional power shattered, Hungary lost more than half of its population and 70 percent of its territory. The Great Depression consequently hit the country very hard, and reliance on trade with Germany (and Italy) to stay afloat during those hardscrabble years precipitated an alliance with the Axis powers during World War II.

Hungary did its best to protect Jewish citizens from deportation during the early years of the war, but in 1944 Germany (after learning that Hungary was secretly negotiating a separate peace with the United States and Britain) occupied the country and began sending Jews to concentration camps in massive numbers. By the end of the war, in addition to the deaths of nearly one million Hungarian soldiers and citizens, more than half a million Hungarian Jews had lost their lives in the Holocaust. According to the Holocaust Memorial Center, approximately one-third of all Jews killed at Auschwitz were Hungarian. Many of my relatives lost their lives in this death camp, my father being the only one of his immediate family to survive its horrors.

Then the Soviets occupied Hungary and established a communist dictatorship. I came into the world at a time (only two years after the end of the war) of immense sadness, widespread poverty, political repression, and cultural confusion. There seemed to be tension everywhere: between Hungarians and Soviets, between "old" Europe and "new" America, between Jews and Roman Catholics. In terms of religion, the enforced communist doctrine of nonbelief attempted to supplant our Christian faith or Jewish orthodoxy. Our loyalties and traditions, indeed our very beliefs, were pushed and pulled in every direction.

These struggles were personified for me, as a young girl, in the tension between my father and mother. Their turbulent relationship and subsequent divorce, so indicative of the instability of the times, precipitated my being sent to the orphanage, where I spent most of the following ten years. For me, the reunion of my parents was the outcome I prayed for the most, as if the anxiety and confusion I sensed everywhere in the culture would be resolved through that one act of love and understanding.

The orphanage seemed like such an enormous and formidable place to me when I was a child. In 1991, when I took my family there, it seemed calm and safe, even quaint. Seen in light of the history of conflicts Hungary had endured, the orphanage seemed to me a symbol of quiet strength, formidable resolve, and protective energy. It was from another time, but the fact that it was still there, still functioning, still providing food, shelter, and education to children without home and family, gave me an immense sense of pride and well-being.

Ironically, the Soviet occupation had recently ended; in fact, the last of the Russian troops had finally left the country only weeks before we arrived in June 1991. Hungary, after decades bouncing between monarchies and fascist or communist dictatorships, was finally emerging as a democratic nation run by a parliament. Freedom, so scarce and fragile during my childhood, had returned to Hungary, and it moved me to my core.

As it was July when we visited Budapest, the orphanage was closed and all the kids were in foster homes for the summer break. We just walked into the courtyard, and I guided the children while Jud got his camera ready. My heart was beating fast as I sat on the stone base of the iron fence, holding Lauren in my lap and hugging Nathan standing next to me. For a moment it truly felt like a dream. I looked at my husband while he took our picture, and he was crying right along with me. These were happy tears we were sharing; tears of vindication and deep gratitude.

Chapter 1
MY FATHER

Tibor Kalman, my father, was born on June 4, 1913, in Esperjes, Hungary, to a very prominent Orthodox Jewish family. They moved to Miskolc for better business opportunities when Dad was four years old, and their hard work paid off. By the time he started school they owned the first and only vinegar factory in Miskolc, along with a chain of photo shops, the first of their kind in Hungary.

Miskolc was an industrial city at the time of my father's birth. Though it wasn't a battleground during World War I, many of its young men were killed fighting in the war, and a large number of civilians also died during that time from a debilitating cholera epidemic. The city suffered serious damage during the final months of World War II, and the postwar years were difficult, but Miskolc maintained its status as the industrial center of northeastern Hungary. These days, Miskolc has established itself as a cultural center as well, sporting many annual art and music events, including the International Opera Festival of Miskolc, which is also known as the Bartók + Opera Festival in honor of Hungary's renowned twentieth-century composer Béla Bartók.

Dad was the youngest of three children. The oldest was my uncle, Odon, who became a successful doctor of internal medicine and also played the violin. Aunt Irene, the middle child, married a doctor and stayed home to raise her two children even though she had a university education. She was a wonderful pianist as well. Dad was the baby of the family, and the most gifted of the three when it came to music. He started playing cello at age five and excelled from the beginning. It was clear to everyone that my father's future was in music, and they made sure that he received the best musical education possible. Initially, Dad took private lessons; later he studied cello in Budapest and graduated from the Royal Franz

Liszt Music Academy and the Vienna Music Conservatory.

My grandfather, Izso Kalman, was also a gifted violin player, and he was my father's biggest fan. They were very close. Grandfather Izso taught my father how to sing and harmonize, which the whole family did on many an occasion from the time Dad was very young. My grandmother, Elaine, was a very smart business-woman, and she basically ran the family business.

My father had an ideal childhood in the city of Miskolc. His family gave him much love and support, and his musical career took off. He performed with the Budapest Philharmonic Orchestra, under such famous conductors as Bruno Walters and Otto Klemperer; and his string quartet performed in Vienna, Austria, and Venice, Italy, as well as numerous venues in Budapest. Life was good. He was a very handsome young man and enjoyed dating young women, who were only too eager to be by his side. But Dad was really married to his cello, and was relentless in pursuing his dream to become a concert cellist.

I loved listening to his stories about practicing his cello eight to ten hours a day (and often much longer when he was getting ready for a concert). He told me that Grandfather would pull up his chair and sit there to watch him practice for hours, just to show his support. Grandmother would often come in to check on him, bringing treats. She would massage his fingers, sore from practicing so many hours. Music played a very important role in the Kalman family, and they spent many evenings singing together and having family concerts.

These precious memories of his loving family gave my father the will to survive the horrors of the Holocaust just a few years later. Nobody could have predicted how much everything would change when Hitler came to power in the early 1930s. The persecution of the Jewish people began in Germany but soon spread to both eastern and western Europe. Hitler, as we know, was determined to wipe out all the Jews, and eventually everyone else he didn't consider a member of the "superior" Aryan race.

Hungary was basically powerless to resist Germany's influence during World War II. Her close proximity and dependence on

German trade all but ensured Hungary would become aligned with the Axis powers. And at first there were benefits, such as newly negotiated territorial borders and financial assistance that helped the country survive the Great Depression. Under economic and political pressure, Hungary officially joined in alliance with Germany in 1940, and we participated in the invasions of Yugoslavia and the Soviet Union.

While fighting the Soviets and suffering increasing losses, Hungary began secret peace negotiations with America and the Allied powers. When Germany became aware of this, they occupied Hungary and began deporting Hungarian Jews by the thousands to concentration camps in Auschwitz and Buchenwald. In spite of this, and the horror stories people soon heard, many of the Jews in Hungary really didn't believe that they would be taken to these camps. But life for Jews in Hungary became increasingly difficult. Everyone had to wear the Star of David on their arm and all businesses with Jewish proprietors were closely monitored. Still, many people remained in denial and continued to conduct their lives as if things were normal.

Auschwitz has become an international symbol of the horrors of the Holocaust; for me and my father it was the place where our relatives were murdered by ruthless anti-Semites. In 1935, after the enactment of the Nuremberg Laws, German Jews were stripped of their citizenship because they didn't share "Germanic or related" blood, and this discrimination escalated into a systematic attempt to eradicate the Jewish race, a policy that was formalized at the Wannsee Conference in 1942. After the Germans occupied Hungary in 1944, Hungarian Jews were deported en masse to the Auschwitz camp, where most perished in the gas chambers.

According to the selection process at the camp, anyone deemed not "fit for work" was immediately put to death, while those that could perform physical labor were sent to nearby labor camps, where they were worked until, in most cases, they literally dropped dead from starvation and fatigue. More Hungarian Jews died at Auschwitz than any other group, with an approximate loss of 438,000. The next-largest group was Polish Jews, of whom

300,000 lost their lives in the camp. It is estimated that one in six Jews murdered in the Holocaust died at Auschwitz.

My grandfather, Izso, died in June 1944, right before my father and his family were taken to this hellish death camp. The men and women were separated, and the children were taken away from their parents. My father was put to work in a labor camp, in Galicia near the Hungarian-Polish border. But the rest of his family was taken straight to the gas chambers. He never saw or heard from them ever again, and didn't find out how they died until after the war was over.

Life in the labor camp was brutal. Prisoners were forced to build railroads in the Hungarian countryside not far from the gas chambers. The only positive thing was that some of my father's former colleagues from the string quartet ended up in the same camp with him. Occasionally they were required to perform at night for the German officers and guards, who craved entertainment. Germans were known for their love of classical music, and, as luck would have it, Dad's gift of playing the cello helped him (and his fellow musicians) receive slightly better treatment than the rest of the men in the camp. Eventually it played a role in their escape from the camp a few months later.

When the Germans began losing the war—after the United States joined the Allies—things got increasingly disorganized and chaotic in the camp. The German soldiers routinely got drunk every night. There were constant changes in leadership as people were either moved to different posts or ran off, afraid of what might happen to them after the war. They knew that once everyone found out about the atrocities done to hundreds of thousands of innocent people, they would be held accountable.

One night, after Dad and his buddies had finished playing their obligatory concert for the intoxicated Germans, many of the guards fell asleep and others just left the camp. This was my father's big chance to escape, and he and the other musicians sneaked out of the camp in the middle of the night.

By this time, in the early days of 1945, the Russians were advancing into eastern Europe as the American troops swept in from the west. My dad and his three friends just kept on walking trying to get as far away from the camp as possible. The second day of their long walk there were shots fired around them, and they ran into an abandoned farmhouse to hide—after all, they were escaped Jewish prisoners and had no idea who was firing the shots.

Then there was a big explosion as an artillery shell hit the house. Dad was injured badly. When he regained consciousness, he was being carried on a wagon covered in blood and suffering excruciating pain in his right arm. The Russian soldiers eventually brought him to a vacant church that had been turned in to a makeshift emergency center. A Russian doctor explained to my father that he was losing too much blood, and for him to survive they needed to amputate his right arm to stop the bleeding. The last thing he remembered was the unbearable pain as his arm was cut off. He remained unconscious for days after. He was thirty-one years old.

The next few months were a nightmare as Dad went through a slow and painful recovery in a local hospital. After he was well enough to be discharged, he made his way back to Miskolc, where he learned that none of his immediate family had survived the concentration camp in Auschwitz. He was now completely alone, with one arm, his beloved family gone, and his life-long dream of being a concert cellist shattered.

After the war was officially over, the Soviet Army occupied Hungary along with most of Eastern Europe For several years after the war, the Soviets used political pressure to ensure that communists would be the governing majority in Russia's neighboring Eastern European countries. In February 1946 the Hungarian monarchy was officially abolished and replaced with the Soviet-controlled Republic of Hungary. After the mutual assistance treaty between Russia and Hungary in 1949, Soviet troops in Hungary became a mainstay until the fall of the Soviet empire in 1991.

When Dad returned to Miskolc, he found the family home destroyed, the vinegar factory bombed out and badly damaged, and most of the photo shops in ruins. The family fortune had been hidden somewhere underground in Miskolc. This was a common practice among the Jewish people when the persecution began. They were trying to protect their assets for family members so they could rebuild their lives in the event they were lucky enough to survive the Holocaust. My father used this money (and sold the family's jewelry) to pay the costs of rebuilding the vinegar factory.

My father had a distant aunt who was, like him, the only survivor of her immediate family in the Holocaust. She owned a very small grocery store in Miskolc, and Dad stayed with her while he rebuilt the vinegar factory, the family home, and his personal life.

One day Dad went to his aunt's store to pick up some groceries. When he was paying for the food he saw a beautiful young girl in her teens at the cash register. The rest, as they say, was history. Gabriella Molnar was a stunning young beauty and Dad was a very handsome man in his prime. It was love at first sight for both of them. The pretty young lady would soon become Dad's wife and my mother.

The famous trio performed all over the country and Europe.

Formal photo of my father when he began performing as a solo cellist with the Budapest Philharmonic Orchestra circa 1938.

Last picture of my father with two arms immediately after arriving at the labor camp. He is smiling, not really knowing what to expect.

The tombstone of my paternal grandfather; the only member of the Kalman family who passed away right before the family was taken to the gas chambers.

The back side of the tombstone shows the list of the names of my father's family killed in the gas chambers of Auschwitz.

The ties that bind across miles, years

Tibor Kalman, right, and Frederic Balazs — partners after four decades.

Fred Balazs and my Father: A lifetime of unbreakable friendship.

Chapter 2
MY MOTHER

Gabriella Molnar, my mother, was born on March 18, 1929 in Debrecen, Hungary. She was the third child out of six. When she was born her parents already had two girls, and soon after her, they had two boys and another girl. Mom never had anything new, only hand-me-downs from her two older sisters. She was closest with the firstborn, Aranyka, and oddly enough both of them married much older men and then divorced, and then married twice more. They also shared the similar trait that their lives were primarily focused on men. It seemed they were unable to live their lives alone.

Mom's birth seemed a prophecy of hard times to come. My grandmother was on her way home from the outdoor village market when she could tell that her baby was coming and there was no stopping it. Grandfather was at work, but fortunately the two older girls, Aranyka and Mandi, were there to help. They were close to the famous Nine Arch bridge when my grandmother could not go any farther, and she lay down under on of the arches where there was shade and some privacy. It was not an easy birth, but it was quick. At that point some good-hearted women came with my two young aunts, and they cut the cord and wrapped my mother in some warm towels. Then somebody came with a wagon to take grandmother home. The next day, the village doctor paid her a visit, but she was already up taking care of her family. Grandmother used to say that the birth was just the forewarning that there wasn't going to be anything easy about raising my mother.

I know Mom got into trouble a lot for not minding, or not telling the truth, or just generally misbehaving. Grandmother always had to be there to rescue her, and the other children often felt that Mom got more attention than they did. It sometimes makes me think of the story of the Prodigal Son in the Bible, who caused so much heartache and pain for his father, yet was still loved and welcomed home regardless of what he had done in the past.

My grandmother, Margit Jassinger, came from a very poor Orthodox Jewish family in Debrecen, Hungary. There she met my grandfather, Miklos Molnar, who was a university graduate and an engineer by profession. He came from a very prominent Roman Catholic Family. Their worlds could not have been more different, but as they say, love is blind and nothing could come between them. They fell in love, and then broke with tradition by getting married without the approval of their families. In the early 1900 it was simply unheard of for an orthodox jewish girl to date or be even in the same room with a man of roman catholic faith

While there had always been a tenuous relationship between Jews and Christians in Europe, the divide grew to its most dangerous level during the twentieth century. "Blood libel" accusations (the baseless claim that Jews were murdering Christians and using their blood in religious rituals) led to the immigration of approximately 175,000 European Jews to America in the mid-twentieth century. Unfortunately, anti-Semitism was also peaking in the United States during these years, with prominent American heroes like Henry Ford and Charles Lindbergh openly supporting fascism and espousing the moral inferiority of the Jewish race. It was even worse, though, in Europe, and the rise of the Nazism brought the hatred between Christians and Jews to a fever pitch.

During these years in Hungary, it was unacceptable that an Orthodox Jewish girl with only an eighth-grade education would marry a well-educated, well-to-do Roman Catholic gentleman. Both were immediately disowned, and they never saw or heard from their parents again. I could never get my grandparents to talk about their parents or the families they had lost.

My grandmother converted to Catholicism long before the war, and my grandfather was Roman Catholic going back several generations. Since she had had no contact with her family for so many years and had become such a devout Christian, nobody knew of her Jewish background. This likely saved her life during the Holocaust.

For the first five years of their marriage, Grandma and Grandpa didn't have children. Grandmother started attending church with Grandpa on Sundays but didn't convert to Christianity at that time. Then, one night, she had a very unusual dream. Here is how she told it to me:

One Sunday we did what we always do; we went to church, and then I was preparing our noon dinner. It was a quiet, ordinary day. I had been feeling something stirring inside of me after years of attending the Catholic Church services. I began to question my Jewish faith, and I wanted to know more about this Jesus person whom the Christians worshipped and the Jewish people denied. Your grandpa and I had long talks about our faiths, but he never pushed me to convert. He was waiting patiently for me to come around.

That particular Sunday night we went to bed and I had the most unusual dream, one as real as anything I ever experienced. In the dream, I was on my way home from our church and it was a very stormy day. I got so lost and I just could not find my way home. It was completely dark and all I could think about was my children waiting for me at home with Grandpa probably worrying about my whereabouts. The more I tried to find my way home, the more lost I got.

I was frantic with fear and the rain was coming down very hard. I was soaking wet, my feet sinking in the muddy road, which slowed me down and made me even more desperate. In my exhausted state, I finally just dropped down on my knees and cried out to Jesus for his help! I vaguely remember saying something like, 'Jesus, if you really exist, please take my hand and help me to get home!' I was sobbing so hard that I thought I was going to die. And then out of nowhere there was this soft light coming from behind me, and in that moment I knew that somehow I was going to be okay. Jesus had heard my plea! I was afraid to turn my head around, but felt a hand touch me and lift me up out of the mud. When I looked up I saw our house with the lights on right ahead of me, and I just walked straight toward our door.

Grandpa was already standing at the door, waiting for me anxiously. I was going to tell him everything that happened to me after I cleaned off all the dirt and mud that covered me from the storm. When I looked down I could not believe my eyes. I was completely clean and dry and there was not a speck of mud or dirt anywhere on me.

I woke up in the middle of the night completely soaked with sweat, and I cried like a baby. Grandpa woke up quite concerned, thinking I must be ill, but I finally calmed down and slowly started telling him about my extraordinary dream. He held me in his arms for a very long time, and during that night I made the decision to convert to Catholicism and give my heart to Jesus. Then I fell into the deepest and most peaceful sleep. The next Sunday I became a Christian and never looked back. Three months later I became pregnant with our first child, Aranyka, and as you know we had five more children after that: Mandika, Gabriella (my mom), Imre, Klarika, and Bela.

A few months after I became a Christian, something else happened that was very unusual. We came home from church, and I was about to start preparing our Sunday noon dinner, but I got this sudden urge to leave the house. I felt I was supposed to go somewhere, so I just picked up my purse and took off. Grandpa was completely perplexed, and decided to follow me. He must have thought that I'd lost my mind! I remember stopping at some house not too far from our home, and without knocking I opened the front door. I saw about a dozen or so people sitting in a circle, and there was an empty chair in the middle of the circle. Then everything went blank for me.

When I came to, I was sitting in the middle of the room in that chair looking at all these people I didn't know. They asked me who I was and where I came from, and I asked them the same thing. It was a relief to see Grandpa standing by the door, but he was as confused as I was, trying to figure out what had just happened. Apparently, this group of Christians had been meeting there every Sunday after church for some time, believing that God/Jesus would send them a spiritual leader. We started meeting with this small group after church every Sunday. Grandfather, who knew how to write shorthand, kept a pretty good record of what was I was saying while I was seemingly asleep in a trance. There was so much I still didn't understand, but I knew that I was just an instrument of our Lord and if what I do helps people, then so be it. I just had to follow the path that God had set before me.

My mother always seemed to be struggling while she was growing up. From what I was able to gather from aunts and uncles back home, she was likely sexually abused as a child, either by my grandfather, or, more likely, some friends of the family. It also could have been somebody in the Catholic Church, perhaps one of the priests. I base this on overhearing some verbal exchanges between my grandmother and grandfather, in which they discussed my mother's lack of willpower (as well as that of Mom's older sister) when it came to resisting the attentions they received from the opposite sex. They were also talking a lot about how they would have to watch out for all the girls in the family and keep them away from some of the clergy in their church. Knowing my grandparents' moral values, I suspect it was someone who was close to the family who molested Mom. I have no other explanation for her behavior regarding her constant need to be with men. As I understand it, this kind of behavior is not unusual for a girl who has been molested as a child. When Mother was growing up, nobody talked about it. Adults had a lot of authority over children, and if you tried to speak up, nobody would have believed you anyway.

It was also hard on my mother's family during the war, especially with four young girls. Rape was very widespread during the World War II years, and was not even considered a serious crime by the Soviet or German military. Of course, Jewish women were particularly vulnerable during the reign of Hitler, and in fact, if a German soldier was found guilty of raping a Jewish woman he would be reprimanded for mixing the races, which was strictly forbidden, but not for the rape itself. For both the German and Soviet armies, rape was used as a weapon of war, and Hungarian women were constantly in danger. It is estimated that the Red Army alone raped upward of two million women over the course of the war and its aftermath, mostly in Eastern Europe and Germany.

Knowing that the Russian and German soldiers were committing these crimes routinely, and with girls as young as twelve, my grandmother would smear shoe polish on her daughters' faces and dressed them in baggy clothes so they would hopefully be ignored. Grandmother told me there were a couple close calls, but with God's grace they were spared that horror. She said the Russian soldiers just looked so young, and often she would feed them because they were cold and hungry. She prayed that would shift their attention away from going after the girls.

Mom never finished high school, but some of her more sophisticated and well-educated male friends exposed her to literature, the arts, and (thanks to my father) classical music, opera, and ballet. As an adult she was closest with my uncle Imre, who had a doctorate in literature and became a poet laureate in Hungary. Imre taught my mother poetry and exposed her to classic writers like Arthur Miller, Thomas Mann, and Anton Chekhov. Steinbeck and Hemingway. Imre and Mom also enjoyed the nightlife in Budapest, and Mom particularly loved to be around members of Imre's famous literary circle.

She had a good heart, but that quality often got her into trouble. I remember a story my grandmother told me: My grandfather had gotten a big promotion as an engineer for the railroad, and to celebrate he had a brand new pair of shoes made. One afternoon as a child, Mom was home alone and a beggar knocked on the door asking for food. He was barefoot and it was winter, and Mom felt so sorry for him that she ran into the bedroom, grabbed grandpa's brand new shoes, and gave them to this poor man. Needless to say, she received a very memorable spanking when my grandfather came home.

My parents were married in the spring of 1946. Dad was thirty-one and Mom was only sixteen. He was a well-educated and well-traveled man, while she was only in her second year of high school. I don't think either of them realized at the time the obstacles they would face because of their age differences and different family and religious backgrounds. Dad was raised in an Orthodox Jewish family and Mom was baptized Roman Catholic.

The marriage was complicated from the beginning. Dad wanted a family right away, but Mom didn't want children at all. Nevertheless, she got pregnant soon after they married, and I was born on April 24, 1947 in Miskolc, Hungary. This was two months before her due date and one month after her eighteenth birthday.

Dad was busy rebuilding the vinegar factory, and he moved his new family into a bigger home where they would have room for more children. Mom did convert to Judaism and tried to please my father, but it was clear from the beginning that she didn't want to be a full-time wife and mother. She was just not emotionally prepared for the responsibility. My grandmother and a nanny took over my care, and that really disappointed Dad. He needed a strong partner and instead found himself with a child bride.

My grandparents had opposed the marriage from the very beginning. The age difference was a big concern, not to mention the different religions. But, ironically, they had done exactly the same thing, my grandfather being from a Roman Catholic family and my grandmother from an Orthodox Jewish one. The age difference between my grandparents was also significant—twelve years as compared to fifteen for my parents. One needed to convert, so Grandma converted to Catholicism and had six children, all raised in the Catholic faith. While they were both disowned by their parents the day they got married, my mother was able to keep in touch with her family after she got married, perhaps because my grandparents identified with her situation even though they opposed the marriage. My grandmother was deeply concerned that, being so young, Mom would not understand the horrors that my father suffered during the war and would not know how to be a supportive partner to my father.

I was almost one year old when the vinegar factory was ready for the grand opening. The day after the grand opening, Dad went to the factory to open for business, only to find that government officials had taken over the building. Unfortunately, by this time Hungary was a Communist country under Soviet occupation, and the party was in the process of taking over all the privately owned businesses. They informed my father that the factory was now officially government property, and he was told to leave. When he asked if he could go in to pick up his work jacket and the briefcase he left in his office, he was not even allowed to do that.

The Soviet Union asserted legal authority to seize private assets from occupied territories. Beginning with the Communist revolution, it became policy for the Russian state to take lands and assets from the nobility and redistribute this wealth among the peasantry. Following the Potsdam Agreement between the primary Allied countries (Great Britain, the United States, and the Soviet Union) in July 1945, which laid out the laws governing Germany's demilitarization and war reparations, the Russians were able to take advantage of loopholes to justify nearly any property seizure they wished under a veneer of legality. For instance, if any company was wholly or in part owned by German or Austrian interests, the seizure of that asset was justified as war reparation. This affected Hungary greatly because many Hungarian companies were partnered with Austrian companies. In any event, this essentially gave the Soviets carte blanche—they could take any property or business they wished and dedicate it to their agenda.

This happened everywhere in Hungary and all over Eastern Europe. Of course, the Russians waited until the factories and other businesses were rebuilt before they took them over. This was a common practice by the Soviets—letting the private businesses do the rebuilding at their own expense so that when the factories were surrendered the government could start operations immediately and reap all the benefits.

My father was again facing an uncertain future, and this time with a young family. Losing the factory—which was the only thing left from his family's business and in which he had invested all the family's assets—was devastating. These were hard times for everybody, and I don't believe that my mother ever fully realized the pressure my father was under. She was a beautiful young woman, but had no idea how to be supportive wife and partner to my father during those trying years.

After losing the factory, Dad moved his young family to Budapest, the largest city and capital of Hungary, where he thought he might have more opportunities to find employment. But Budapest was struggling to rebuild after the war, and life was very hard there, too. The city had suffered major damage and casualties in the last year of the war, after Germany occupied Hungary. In February 1945, the city was nearly destroyed in the Battle of Budapest. After being subjected to massive air raids by the Allied forces and ground fighting between attacking Soviet forces and defending Hungarian or German forces, nearly forty thousand civilians lost their lives, and every bridge in the city was destroyed.

I was two years old when we moved to Budapest. By this time my parents' marriage was floundering. Dad wasn't getting the support he needed from my mother, and she had no concept of the magnitude of his losses—emotionally, physically, and financially. He had lost his entire family, he had lost the factory (and the family money he used to rebuild it), and he had lost his right arm and with it his dreams of becoming a concert cellist. Now even his marriage was falling apart and he did not know where to turn next.

Dad was beginning to lose hope of being able to start over again. As luck would have it—I would rather say it was God's intervention—he ran into an old friend in Budapest one afternoon when he was just taking a walk and wondering how to go on, almost ready to give up the fight to survive. His friend, Katinka Daniel, a respected piano teacher, knew my father from the time when they were both studying at the Budapest Music Academy. Her husband, Dr. Erno Daniel, was a young conductor.

When Katinka saw Dad she was overjoyed that he was alive and had survived persecution during the war. Katinka had a lot to tell my father, also. Her beloved husband, Erno, left Hungary to go west just before the war ended, with the promise to build a better life for her and their two children in America. Katinka was left by herself to raise her children alone, but her faith was strong and she knew her husband would keep his word and that they would eventually reunite. They did, but it took twelve years.

The friendship between Katinka and my father came at the

right time, and they helped each other a lot. Dad was obviously struggling, but Katinka, a deeply religious Christian woman, was very encouraging. She helped my father get a job teaching cello to young students, and he also started conducting the Hungarian Communist Party Chorus, with Katinka accompanying him on piano. During this time Dad also went back to school and got his master's degree in music. Eventually he became one of the most well-known and highly regarded cello teachers in the country, and his close friendship with the Daniel family lasted throughout their lives.

The newlyweds: mom and dad.

Picture of the young bride.

One of my favorite pictures of my handsome dad.

First year of marriage; still a happy couple before my early arrival.

Last family photo taken on April 25, 1949; the day after my second birthday. The marriage was already in trouble.

The only picture of my maternal grandmother and grandfather together; they were married almost 60 years.

Grandmother, dressed for church.

Last picture of my grandmother, the year before
she passed away.

Chapter 3
MY CHILDHOOD

My full birth name was Ildiko Judit Kalman. My mother named me Ildiko after the last wife of Attila the Hun, who, as legend has it, was the sister of the western emperor Valentinian III. Some said that the teenage bride Ildiko killed Attila for forcing her into the marriage. The name is certainly Germanic in origin, sharing the same root with Hildegard and Hildchen, and has come to mean "fighter" or "fierce warrior." Considering the trials of my life in Hungary, I feel this is quite appropriate, and I am proud that my name is a symbol of the strength I needed to survive those difficult years. My middle name, Judit, was in honor of my father's niece (the daughter of his sister, Irene) who perished at Auschwitz.

According to my grandmother, I surprised everyone by arriving two months earlier than expected. She would often joke that I was in such a hurry to enter this world, and that nothing much has changed since that time. I still tend to be in a hurry in everything I do. I like to be early whenever possible, especially when I promise to be somewhere for our children; and I am fanatical about arriving early at airports!

Since I was premature, things didn't look too good for me at first. Mom told me that I was not a pretty baby, and that at first she didn't want my father to see me because she was afraid he would not believe that I was his child. I think she really had no idea how to take care of me. Mom had no interest in nursing me at all, so we had a nanny with enough milk for babies. She fed me while she was nursing her own baby, too. I was a sickly infant, very colicky, and didn't grow at the normal rate. My grandmother, having raised six children, quickly realized that I wasn't getting enough nutrition, and this was why I wasn't growing and kept losing weight. According to my folks, I cried constantly and slept very little. For a while it was questionable whether I was going to survive. The family doctor kept giving me shots to keep me alive, but that is not what I needed.

One day my feisty grandmother happened to visit when our doctor was at our house administering one of my many shots. Of course, I was crying, and according to Grandmother it was mostly from hunger. She loved to tell me the story of the time she literally threw the doctor out of the house because he was giving me shots and collecting money from my parents when all I needed was some food. Grandma then brought in a live chicken and some fresh vegetables from her garden. She prepared a big container of chicken soup, poured it through a strainer, and put the nutritious liquid in a bottle. She fed me and for the first time I slept more than twenty-four hours. When I finally woke up, I didn't cry. From that moment on Grandma took over my care and I began to grow at a fast pace.

Six months later my grandmother ran into our former family doctor when she was taking me for a walk, and he did not recognize me at all, confusing me with my cousin Agi, who was only ten days older than me. Within a couple of months under my loving grandmother's care I had filled out, my eyes changed from brown to blue, and my dark hair slowly fell out and was replaced with blond curls (I did begin to resemble Agi, as we were both blond children). Until the end of her life my grandmother swore that her chicken soup saved my life. To this day, chicken soup is still one of my favorite foods.

We moved into one of the nicer neighborhoods in Budapest in 1949. Our address was 84 Vaci Street. Our flat was on the fourth floor, and was nicely furnished as I recall. From our window I could see Gellert Mountain with the Freedom Statue, where they had fireworks for Worker's Day every May 1. My kindergarten was just a few blocks away, as were the Danube River and the Freedom Bridge. Once we moved to Budapest, we no longer had domestic help the way we had in Miskolc, and my mother did not adjust well to her new circumstances. She was not willing to take on the responsibility of being a supportive wife to my father and mother to me. She was then twenty years old.

Dad began to teach cello, and he became the head conductor for the Hungarian Communist Party Chorus. We had a lot of company in the evenings, mostly musicians who were either playing in the Budapest Symphony or teaching music like my father. Dad worked very long hours, and money was tight. Everyone was just trying to survive under the new Communist regime. I clearly remember the constant quarrels between Mom and Dad each night after the guests left. I could tell something was very wrong, but I didn't really understand any of it. Somehow, though, I suspected that my parents might have cheated on each other, and I was filled with fear that they might abandon me. I could tell that my father was angry with my mother for not taking care of me, while she would make excuses and blame Dad for my existence. Clearly, motherhood was not her calling.

In the winter of 1951, I got very sick with the mumps and was running a very high fever. I still remember the nice, elderly family doctor who came and gave me medication. I was happy when he came over because my parents wouldn't quarrel in front of him. One particular night I woke up from a feverish sleep and heard the yelling between Mom and Dad. It was frightening. The next thing I remember, Dad stormed out of the apartment and left. Mom was crying, and then minutes later she grabbed her purse and took off as well.

Thank goodness they left all the lights on. I got out of bed to run after them, but the door was locked. This was exactly what I feared the most—that I would be left alone without my parents. In my confused state I imagined all sorts of frightening things. I was sure that I was going to die and nobody would care. I started crying, and I must have cried for so long and so loud that our next-door neighbor heard me and became concerned. He called the building manager who came up with his wife. They broke the lock on the door to our flat and stayed with me until the morning. I remember that when my parents finally did return it was getting light outside. This feeling of being left alone so often at such a young age (I was then four) really affected me as I began raising my own children. It became almost an obsession never to leave them alone, especially our daughter. Even when they were away at college I was always asking them if they were alone. I just could not relax until I was certain that they had a friend, a roommate, or someone with them.

When I asked my parents why they left me, Dad told me he thought Mom would stay with me. Mom said she thought she would only be gone a short time. The truth is, they were busy dealing with their own issues and forgot about me. When their fighting continued it became obvious to me that both of them spent that night with other people And my simple existence made their lives a lot more complicated. To this day I don't know how I knew this, but somehow I did. Sadly, I learned later that my suspicions were correct. During their constant quarrels I recognized some of the names of the people with whom they suspected each other of being unfaithful. It broke my heart, and I just wanted to disappear. Did my mother and father ever love each other?

The following week Dad moved out of our home and into a one-bedroom studio apartment not far from our Vaci Street flat. He left everything behind for my mother. He took only his clothes and the grand piano and music books that he needed for his teaching jobs. The divorce proceedings were concluded fairly quickly. Mom cried a lot and kept asking me to ask Dad to come back home. A few times I made an attempt to convince him to try again, but he was very bitter and wouldn't even talk to me about Mom. He tried very hard never to look back but at the same time did his very best to take care of me under these difficult circumstances. He worked long hours, six to seven days a week, and I was grateful to be with him from early in the morning to late in the evening. During the week Dad took me to kindergarten in the morning, picked me up at six o'clock and I stayed with him at his school until he finished teaching usually around ten o'clock at night. He was teaching or performing with his chorus most weekends but he always took me with him. It meant a lot to me that he never left me alone, he was always on time to pick me up from kindergarten and he made me feel that I was important to him.

During my preschool and kindergarten years, I was always the last kid to be picked up after school when it was my mother's turn (if she even came at all). Most of the time, the person who would come for me was my father. Mom rarely made it, and when she did, it was always very late and I would often be out on the street waiting for her after the school closed at six in the evening. Sometimes I just walked home because I was too embarrassed to be the last one left at school all the time. I would make up stories about how my mother had to work and that was why she could not come and get me. In truth, I never knew where she was. Sometimes the neighbors would feel sorry for me and invite me into their flats to wait for Mom to show up. I was very grateful for their kindness, especially in the freezing winter when being on the street was no fun at all.

When I was walking around on the streets looking for my mother, it never occurred to me that I might be molested or that somebody could really hurt me. Sometimes, when I had no place to go, I would take the streetcar to be with my grandmother, who always welcomed me with so much love and concern. I knew I would be safe with her and my grandfather. We would always pray together for my mother and father. Of course, I always prayed for the impossible: that my parents would one day reconcile so that we could become a normal family.

I spent a lot of time sitting on the staircase by our front door until Mom came home. Sadly, she usually had a male companion with her, so even when she did come home I felt like I was in the way most of the time. Men were attracted to my mother like bees to honey. She was very beautiful and had the most amazing laugh. Whenever I was with her I always noticed how men just looked at her in a way that made me feel very uncomfortable. I sensed that my presence was not always welcome. Mom loved all the attention from the opposite sex and seeking that attention consumed her life.

Looking back now, I realize that my mother had no idea what I was feeling. She was totally absorbed in her own life and her own needs, and had no knowledge of all the tears I shed through so many nights while she was sleeping with different men. I tried hard to be a good kid, and I could never understand why I wasn't wanted by my own mother. I was grateful that I at least I had my father, who never broke a promise to me. Although he was not overly affectionate, whenever it was his turn to take care of me, he never let me down. I was vaguely aware that my father also had some lady friends, but it never interfered with his parental responsibilities.

Dad worked long hours teaching cello. Often, his days began at 8:00 a.m. and didn't end until 10:00 p.m. He often picked me up from kindergarten at six in the evening and took me back to the school where he was giving cello lessons to his gifted students late into the night. We would have supper in his tiny studio apartment. Our meals were very simple. We usually drank tea with some day-old bread with dried salami and maybe an apple, if they were in season. I was just happy because I had my dad all to myself. I was also eager to help my father in any way I could so I could stay with him longer. I began helping him wash his socks and undergarments in a small sink by his room after I saw him struggling to do this simple task with one hand. I always helped him fix our supper and cleaned up afterward so I could prove to him that I was useful and could take care of things around his place.

I used to wonder why the divorce judge didn't award custody of me to my dad, since he did his best to look after me. It never occurred to me that the judge looked at him and saw a man with one arm who worked long hours trying to make ends meet. Dad was living in a small one-room apartment, sharing a common bathroom with three other tenants. Though this was not ideal for a little girl at age five, obviously the judge didn't know that my father could do more with his one arm than most people could with two.

Mom got a job at a café in Budapest and started to make some money. I knew she got good tips from male customers because she was attractive and fun to be around. She also received child support from my father, which she apparently spent mostly on new clothes and going out with friends. I don't believe she did that to hurt me in any way; she was just young and irresponsible. I also think she simply wanted to be independent and enjoy her life. She never finished high school but was curious, smart, and eager to learn about the world around her. She was young and beautiful and loved all the attention she got because men were very attracted to her. Although her formal education was not completed, she became knowledgeable about classical music, opera, theater, and poetry and loved to read.

She met her second husband while working at the café in Budapest. He was everything my mother wanted at the time. He was good-looking and well educated, very sophisticated in my mother's eyes. She became totally obsessed with this man. His name was George, and he took Mom to the theater, opera, poetry readings, and the horse races (later I learned he was addicted to both gambling and sex). Unfortunately, this relationship hastened a long downward spiral for my mom.

I remember always asking my father to let me live with him because it was unbearable when George was around. I was losing my mother completely to this man. I also started noticing that we had less and less furniture in our flat. I learned later that Mom had started to sell some of the furniture, giving the money to George to feed his gambling habit.

In our one-bedroom flat there was very little room for me, and it was apparent that George didn't particularly like having me around. Often I would take the long bus ride to the suburbs of Budapest where my grandmother and grandfather lived, just to get away from him. I was too embarrassed to tell my father all the things that went on between my mother and George at home, but I was always asking Dad to take me to his place. I never complained about his long working hours as long as I could be there with him.

One day my father sat me down and told me that things needed to change so I would have more stability in my life. He told me it was very important that I get a good education so I could be successful when I grew up. He said that he had arranged for me to move into the Jewish Orphanage in Budapest in the fall of 1953. Since technically I was not an orphan, I was getting some special considerations and Dad would pay a nominal fee for my keep. He was allowed to come to see me twice a week to give me cello lessons, which I was about to start during my first year in school. He also promised me that every summer when school was out we would spend our vacations together.

This was a very confusing time for me. I thought, *If I have a mother and father, why do I have to be in an orphanage? What have I done that my parents don't want me to be around? Why don't they love me?* I also wondered why, if I was baptized Roman Catholic, I was going to a Jewish orphanage. I was certain that there had to be something wrong with me. Was I being punished for something? I spent so many sleepless nights praying and wondering what I could do so my mom and dad would get back together again and want to be with me.

When my mother found out that Dad was enrolling me in the Jewish Orphanage, she became very upset. For a very brief moment I thought she might fight for me and would decide to look after me after all. Sadly, I think that she was upset because she was about to lose the child support that Dad paid her for my care. After I moved into the orphanage these payments would no longer be required, and she would lose part of her monthly income.

I recall my last Christmas at home on Vaci Street before moving into the orphanage. Mom and I were decorating the tree with George. My father was coming over to visit and celebrate Christmas with us in the afternoon, and I was excited and nervous because he was going to meet George, whom I hated with a passion. This man was destroying my secret dream that somehow my parents would get back together and we would be a normal family once again. I was also sad for my father because I didn't know how he would feel seeing my mother so close to another man in the same home which they had shared together.

When my father arrived I was overjoyed. I just ran into his arms and hung on for dear life. He had a little box for me, and in it was a beautiful little Danish doll. The minute I took the doll out of the box I loved it more than anything in the world. That Danish doll was going to be my most special possession.

There was also a beautiful doll from France under the tree in a big box. Mom said the doll was a special gift from George to me. Now, it was very important to me that my father knew how much I loathed George and wanted to get away from him. I also wanted my mother to know that I hated the French doll and didn't want to stay with her and George. So I took their fancy doll and tore the clothes from her body, pulled her head off, and literally destroyed her within seconds.

After my father left I got spanked for ruining the French doll, but frankly, I didn't care. I just had to do something to show my anger and pain. I also intuited that the French doll was not a gift from George, that really Mom had bought it and told me it was from him in an effort to get me to like him. Unfortunately, George stayed in my mother's life for many years. Mom told me, when I was an adult, that the physical attraction between them was so powerful that she simply didn't have the willpower to leave him. Even after she lost her home and everything that my father left for her, she kept George in her life for a very long time.

The little Danish doll my father gave me was my treasured toy for many years. She was my friend, and I took her with me everywhere. When I moved into the orphanage I took her to my grandmother's place for safekeeping, so nothing would happen to her. Every time I stayed with Grandma I would play with my little Danish doll for hours on end. She was dressed in the traditional Danish clothing with lots of underskirts, a printed blouse, a vest, a colorful apron, and a traditional Danish hat. She had lace socks and clogs. Her beautiful blond hair was braided and long. I would redo her hair and redesign her clothes over and over.

I made many outfits out of her underskirts and apron and was always trying to come up with different looks. Grandmother used to watch me and say, "I wonder what you are going to be when you grow up?" Little did I know (and I never would have dreamed it then) that most of my professional life would be spent in the fashion industry, dressing people, doing runway shows, and making regular fashion presentations on a popular morning television program in San Francisco!

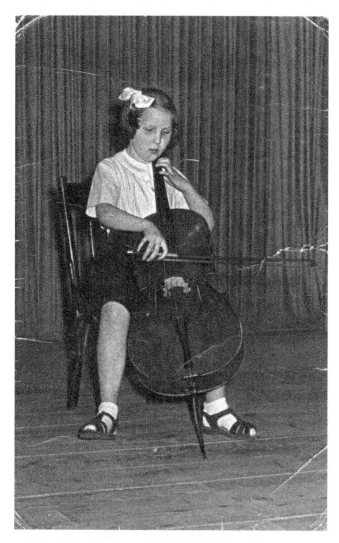

My first solo performance during one of the
fundraiser events for the Orphanage.

My class mates from middle school. My best friend Bea is in the second row, fourth from the right; I am in the last row second from the left.

Picture from second grade in 1954.

Chapter 4
THE ORPHANAGE

In September 1953 my father moved me into the orphanage, and it was to be my home for most of the next ten years. It was on Delibab Street, just on the outskirts of the famous City Park. It was a big yellow building with a tall wrought-iron fence surrounding it. The view from the courtyard was very nice, overlooking the statues of Hungarian kings, which stood in a half-circle on what is appropriately called Heroes Square. On one side of the square was the world-famous Hungarian National Art Museum, and on the other was the Museum of Modern Art. I spent many hours in those museums on school field trips.

To my surprise, Mom did come to see me the day I moved into my new home. For a moment I thought maybe my parents were feeling sorry for me and had decided I didn't really belong in an orphanage after all. Instead, they began to argue again about everything, and it escalated as usual. They said a lot of hurtful things to each other, and it was embarrassing and uncomfortable. Mom kept screaming at my father that there was no reason for me to be in the orphanage, and Dad kept saying that she was not fit to be my mother. I felt that my heart was going to break. They were arguing in front of me as if I didn't exist. I still remember having the same thoughts I had before: *Have they ever really loved each other? Do they really love me?* It seemed to me that I was always the problem.

I was sobbing uncontrollably and begged Dad not to leave me, but he kept assuring me that this was the right place for me to be for now, that this was a better situation for me than being on the street waiting for Mom to come home, or sitting in a classroom late into the night waiting for him to finish teaching. He explained to me that I needed stability and structure in my life and that, more than anything, I needed to be in a place where I was safe. I was only six years old, and I was trying really hard to understand and accept my new life. In my heart all I felt was complete rejection. And then it was time to say good-bye. My mother promised she would get me out of this place soon, but she never did. In fact, she hardly ever came to see me.

The Jewish Orphanage was supported by Holocaust survivors in Budapest as well as people who had emigrated from Hungary to Israel or the United States before the German occupation. This was an Orthodox Jewish institution. The headmistress was named Aunt Olga. Her office was on the first floor. She seemed stern and cold to me (and I thought at the time that she was probably the most unattractive-looking woman I have ever seen). Throughout my time at the orphanage I was scared to death of her.

Aunt Olga knew my father and spoke of him with great respect. Everyone seemed to know Dad, who by this time was making a name for himself as a noteworthy cello teacher. He made arrangements with Aunt Olga to see me on Wednesdays and Sundays to give me cello lessons, and this was when he surprised me with my first cello. I started dreaming about becoming a great cellist. I thought if I worked hard the way he did I could fulfill the dream of my father. I could bring back to him something so valuable that he had lost, and also make him proud of me.

For a long time I was terribly lonely in the orphanage; I just could not make friends with anyone. I remember looking around the courtyard and seeing many girls of all ages running around playing games, but no one seemed to pay any attention to me. Looking back, I think I know why that happened. I wasn't an orphan like nearly all the other children. Also, though my hair had grown darker by then, I noticed that I was the only blond-haired, blue-eyed kid out of eighty-five girls. Everyone else had dark brown or black curly hair, so I just stuck out. They used to tease me nonstop about my looks. The first couple of years I cried myself to sleep almost every night.

Then, when I was in third grade, Frank came to the orphanage. She soon became my very best friend. Our friendship helped both of us to get through those tough times. We had a lot in common: like me, she wasn't an orphan. Her mom was not in good health, and her dad just disappeared one day, leaving home to pick up a pack of cigarettes and never coming back. During the early fifties it was not unusual for people simply to vanish for no apparent reason. The KGB controlled everything, and you never knew who was listening in to your conversations.

Bea and I were complete opposites in looks. She was skinny and sick all the time with asthma. She had very thick brown hair, light olive skin, and big brown almond-shaped eyes. I was lily-white with rosy cheeks, plump and healthy-looking. But Bea and I loved all the same things. We would make up stories about what we would do when we left the orphanage. We had big dreams for our future.

We were lucky because Bea sat next to me in the study room in the orphanage and her bed was also assigned next to mine. We studied together and loved reading, theater, and movies. We started a scrapbook about all of our favorite actors and actresses. We were definitely star-struck! We were completely infatuated with the same actors and imagined what we would say if we ever met them. We created our own fantasy world and had a lot of innocent fun.

We also started writing a daily diary. I think we got our inspiration from the book *The Diary of Anne Frank.* We both instinctively knew that we lived in unusual times that should be recorded. We would often compare our entries and share our most secret thoughts and dreams. And we shed many tears talking about our lives, yet we could also make each other laugh and forget about our often difficult daily reality.

We used to save every penny to buy tickets to the movies or theater. We talked a lot about going to America, where it seemed everybody wanted to go. In school, however, we were taught that America was evil and that it was about rich people taking advantage of poor people. We were brainwashed with daily dogma from *The Communist Manifesto* that the only way to succeed was to support the Communist Party, where everybody was equal and had the same rights.

We were always told that we had to give everything to the Soviet Union because they "liberated" us from the Nazis and we owed them our freedom. We studied the life of Stalin, Lenin, and Marx in school, and their statues were displayed everywhere. We had red stars on every building and all the children were required to become pioneers, members of a youth Communist organization. All of us had to wear a red kerchief around our necks showing our solidarity with the Soviet Union. Our streets were renamed after "Soviet heroes."

Under Communist rule there was no freedom of religion, though at the Jewish orphanage we had religious instruction weekly. In classes, however, the story was completely different. Both Bea and I believed deeply in God, but in school God was never mentioned, as if He didn't exist. In books and poems the word *God* was never capitalized, and when we asked the teacher why God's name wasn't written with a capital G she answered, without blinking an eye, "Because there is no God." Then we saw that very same teacher in the Jewish temple the following Friday at the evening services. We were so indoctrinated with the Communist ideology that we just accepted these double standards as a way of life.

There was one thing we never understood, though. If America was so bad, then why did people want to go there? If the Soviet occupation was so great, then why were people always talking about leaving Hungary to go west for a better life? Bea and I would try to see every American movie, and we would dream about this other world. Even though we knew nothing about it, we both knew we wanted to go there!

The schedule at the orphanage was like being in the military. We wore uniforms to school, but underneath we had to wear dresses made by the in-house seamstress at the orphanage. Everybody had a number that was sewn into our towels and our clothes. I was number 11. We attended public school, and we were always so embarrassed about our clothing because everyone knew that we were the kids from the Jewish orphanage. I remember how humiliated I felt because nobody in school wanted to be friends with us. Even though the war was over, Jews were merely tolerated but not particularly liked. Anti-Semitism was rampant in Hungary and all over Eastern Europe, but nobody talked openly about it.

We had to wake up every morning at six o'clock sharp. Usually, a supervisor would be at the door of the large bedroom where most of us slept. They would have a bucket of cold water ready in case someone decided not to jump out of bed immediately. I tried always to be up early to avoid the cold water treatment!

We had to line up at the communal bathroom sinks to wash our faces, brush our teeth, and then be dressed by 6:30 a.m. Beds had to be made neatly, and then we lined up for breakfast. We had this long main dining room in the basement where we ate at assigned seats, usually decided by what grade we were in school. Breakfast was always the same: coffee with milk and a thick slice of bread (sometimes buttered). It ended at 7:00 a.m., and then we had to go back upstairs to get our school bags, snacks, and coats. After that we lined up downstairs for roll call at 7:15 a.m. We then walked to the nearby public school, which started promptly at 8:00 a.m.

There was an incident that happened one morning at roll call that I could not forget, mainly because it involved my best friend, Bea. We were not allowed to have bangs, and our hair had to be completely out of our faces. Bea did have bangs, but she carefully combed it under her cap, secured with some hairpins. Her hair, however, was very thick in texture and hard to control. She was trying to hide her bangs to get through roll call. Unfortunately, this particular morning her hair would not cooperate and her bangs slipped out just as we were being checked. Aunt Olga was livid and proceeded to get scissors and cut Bea's bangs completely off. It was a miserable scene. Bea cried, and I cried with her. Oh, how I hated that woman in that moment! To this day I still don't understand what she had against bangs; I thought they looked really pretty on Bea.

We got out of school at 2:00 p.m., and then we walked back to the orphanage and had our main meal in the dining room. It was a regular meal with soup, vegetables or potatoes, and sometimes meat or a stew. Then it was time to do homework until 7:00 p.m. All our assigned work was always checked by our supervisor before we finished for the day. At 7:30 we had supper, which usually consisted of hot tea and some buttered bread. Then we had playtime, but I usually took this opportunity to practice my cello. At 9:00 it was bedtime.

There was a temple in the orphanage building that we attended every Friday night and Saturday morning. We also had religious instruction every Wednesday evening, taught by the wife of the rabbi who conducted the services on Fridays and Saturdays. Her name was Aunt Margaret, and she was a wonderful storyteller. I always looked forward to Wednesdays, when I would see my father in the afternoon for cello lessons and would then be with Aunt Margaret in the evening.

I loved being in our temple. It was the place where I practiced my cello and got to spend time alone with my father. I still remember the special smell in the temple, a combination of the fragrance of candles, the dark oak pews, and the old Hebrew prayer books combined. I always felt safe there.

It was a very spiritual experience practicing my cello on the podium where the rabbi gave his sermon every week. There were two large oil paintings in the temple covering the walls facing the pews. One of them was the painting of Moses parting the Red Sea as the Jews were escaping from forty years of captivity in Egypt. The other painting was of Moses with the burning bush. I always practiced my cello as close to these paintings as I could because they made me feel protected and safe. I felt as if a guardian angel were watching over me when I looked at them. I used to pretend there was a big audience in the temple, and it definitely helped me to be less nervous when I later actually started performing in front of larger audiences.

The food in the orphanage was prepared in the Jewish Orthodox tradition, but I never liked it much. We had to say our prayers in Hebrew before every meal. Our supervisors would walk around and watch us eat until we finished our meal. We were not allowed to leave until our plates were completely empty. Most Fridays we had liver and some kind of grits that I simply could not swallow. When the supervisors weren't looking, Bea and I would wrap the liver in our napkins, hide it in our apron pockets, and then flush it down the toilet as soon as we left the dining room. I remember thinking that if I ever got out of there my lips would never touch liver ever again. I have kept that promise!

We bathed in a large communal bath twice a week. There were eight tubs in the basement bathroom, and two girls were assigned to share each tub. Bea and I hated this weekly ritual, and at first I was terrified and so ashamed of being naked in front of the other girls. Our supervisors were standing at the door watching us. To this day I am still shy and do not like to get undressed in front of other people. It was very difficult having no privacy, especially when I became a teenager.

Other than Bea's friendship, what got me thru these years was my father's visits twice a week and the time I spent during holidays at Grandma's place. She always welcomed me with open arms even though they lived on such meager funds. I felt safe and loved when I was around her. I was grateful that I had someplace to go in the summer when most of the children in the orphanage were sent to various foster homes.

Once, I was sent on an errand to go to the headquarters of our Jewish synagogue, which was not far from where Mom lived at the time. I suddenly had a powerful urge to take a detour and go see her. I was afraid that I might get into trouble if someone found out, but I just could not stop myself. There was a voice in my head that kept urging me to go and see her. I had no idea if she would even be home. I know now that it was probably my guardian angel guiding me.

I was totally unprepared for what I found when I entered her unlocked flat. The only furniture left in the room was a single bed. Mom was lying on the bed, crying. She looked very sick and was wearing only a gray skirt and a sleeveless burgundy-colored top— and this was during the winter months. The room was freezing cold, and I could tell that something was terribly wrong. She was begging for help. Terrified, I ran to the apartment of the building manager and asked him to call an ambulance. Fortunately, there was a hospital only three blocks from where she lived. I then called my grandmother and asked her to come right away. My grandparents lived in a village called Jaszvenyszaru, not too far from Budapest, which at the time was only a short train ride away. With a very heavy heart I watched as the ambulance took my mother away.

I was quite late getting back to the orphanage, and could not imagine what story I was going to come up with to explain my tardiness. Thankfully, no one asked me anything, which was most unusual because we usually had to account for our time right down to the minute. I just knew that it had to be a little angel who was watching over me, and over my mother, too.

My grandmother came by the orphanage that weekend to let me know that Mom was doing a lot better. Then Grandma and Grandpa decided to move back from the country to live with Mom for a while and help her get back on her feet. As it turned out, Mom was pregnant and in labor when I stopped by. The child was a boy who was badly deformed, and he died just a few minutes after he was born. I learned later that this baby was a product of her second marriage, with George. At that time, Mom suffered a nervous breakdown and was sent to a sanatorium for a few months to recover. It was very difficult for me, not being able to share this with anyone. She could have died!

My mother and her third husband Gyula in front of
the Eastern Train Station in downtown Budapest.

I am standing in front of the school which I attended for eight years.

Standing at the side gate, this time looking in from the outside.

The orphanage as it looks today—now a five-star boutique hotel called the "Mirage Hotel."

Another view of the orphanage as it appears today. The lower row of windows are where our bedrooms were located.

Chapter 5
THE REVOLUTION

L ife in the orphanage eventually became routine. Slowly I accepted the fact that it was to be my home, at least for a while. Then, on October 23, 1956, the revolution broke out in Hungary, and everything changed. I was nine years old. At the time I really didn't understand the magnitude of what was happening, though I remember hearing before the revolution that people had been disappearing. Basically, anyone who did not openly sympathize with the new regime was called in for questioning at the Communist Party headquarters. They were often tortured, thrown in jail, or simply vanished.

I remember that during the period of Soviet domination there were always shortages of everything. The markets were always running out of bread, milk, sugar, and salt. Putting butter on anything was a luxury. Our delicious Hungarian bread was replaced with dark bread we got from Russia, which was almost inedible. I still remember taking out big chunks of salt that were baked into the bread. The Russians exported our wheat, our cattle, and most of our fine agricultural harvest, and replaced them with their own substandard products.

The grocery stores were always empty. Standing in line for milk, bread, and eggs was part of our daily lives. People were very unhappy, and there was a lot of whispering about some kind of a revolt.

The Hungarian Revolution of 1956, which received international attention, began in the universities. At a march in Budapest, when students attempted to issue demands to the Soviet-backed government via the public radio station, the state police fired on the crowd that was gathered in front of the Magyar (Hungarian) Radio building. A student was killed, and word spread rapidly throughout Budapest, which erupted in violent confrontation with the communists. Soon most of Hungary was supporting the "freedom fighters," and the revolution quickly toppled the puppet Hungarian People's Republic.

At first Russia announced a sort of surrender, claiming they would negotiate the withdrawal of their troops from Hungary, but after a short time they reversed course and decided to crush us. On November 4 additional units of the Soviet army stormed into Budapest and other Hungarian cities, and by November 10 the battle had ended with the defeat of the Hungarian freedom fighters. Several thousand Hungarians died in the revolution, and more than two hundred thousand people fled the country. In the months following, thousands more were imprisoned, deported, or executed.

For me, the morning of the revolution began like any other day. We went to school, but on the way home we noticed a lot of trucks with young university students crowded on top, waving the Hungarian flag and shouting, "Russians go home!" I remember thinking, *Why would we want them to go home if they were our so called "liberators"?* When we got back to the orphanage, our supervisors were glued to the radio and were whispering to one another. By the evening we were told that if anyone had a place to go they should leave, just in case our building got attacked.

It was about 7:00 p.m. when I left the orphanage to go to my mother's place. My father lived much farther away and I was told to avoid certain areas that had become very dangerous. By this time there was complete chaos all over the city. All the streetcars and buses had stopped operating, so I was on foot, trying to stay on side streets to avoid the mobs. At one point, a guy jumped out of his truck, pulled the red kerchief off my neck, and yelled, "Don't wear that thing around your neck because it will get you killed!" I was completely confused and burst into tears. The red kerchief had been a symbol of freedom even as early as that morning! What had changed?

It took two very long hours to get to my mom's place. My grandma was in complete panic when I arrived. Apparently, my mother was on her way to the orphanage to get me. There were rumors everywhere that the Jews were again in danger and might be deported. My grandparents and I were trying to listen to the news on the radio, but we got nothing but static. We did manage to hear something about taking our country back and chasing the Soviet occupiers out of Hungary. We were terribly worried about my mother because we heard gunshots everywhere. Thankfully, she returned home safely by midnight.

By the next day, the Hungarian revolutionaries had taken over the radio station and we heard from the leader of the revolt, Imre Nagy. He assured us that we would win the revolution, that we would banish the Soviet occupation once and for all, and that our country would finally be free and independent of any foreign influence.

We were not allowed to go outside for several days, and often we had to go down to the basement when we heard the siren warning of approaching Soviet tanks. Rumors were going around that the Russians were coming in full force to quash the revolution. We heard that anyone opposing the Soviet occupation would go to jail or be killed. This was definitely bad news for us, as both of my uncles were fighting with our freedom fighters.

On Tuesday, November 20, 1956, after the failure of the revolution and with the shooting finally slowing down, my father came and took me to his place. He told my mom that he wanted to spend some time with me because he was concerned that I wasn't practicing my cello. He also said that we would go out to the countryside to bring back some meat and other food supplies. That sounded really good because we had very little to eat and hadn't had any meat for weeks. With that I said good-bye to my mother and grandparents and left with my father. I remember holding his hand when we were walking to his place. I was so happy he had risked his life to come and get me.

When we got to his place, Dad fixed our usual meal of some old bread, dry salami, and hot tea. He told me that we had to go to sleep right after supper because we were leaving for the countryside very early the next morning to get some meat to bring home. I believed him. I thought it was odd that he didn't ask me to practice my cello while we were there, but I didn't ask any questions.

I tried to go to sleep on the sofa bed, but I kept waking up. At one point I saw my father sitting under a very dim light as he sewed some money into the lining of his big leather coat. As I watched him sewing with one arm, I couldn't believe his concentration and skill. I watched with great admiration as he held the needle in his teeth and threaded it. Then he held his coat in his teeth and sewed the money inside the lining. I wanted to help him so badly that night, but something told me that I was not supposed to see what he was doing. I also wondered why he was hiding money inside his coat.

He got me up at 4:00 a.m., and when we went downstairs there was a big truck waiting for us on the street. When I climbed into the truck I saw that it was it was full of people. I counted them — thirty people exactly, including us. Were they all going to the country to get some food? It was still very dark outside, and the whole city seemed to be asleep. Dad told me to be very quiet. I tried to listen to what people were talking about and found it interesting that nobody was talking about all the meat and other food supplies they were going to buy.

We traveled for many hours and arrived in the city of Vesprem late in the afternoon. I vaguely remembered having heard that people used this city as one of the stops when they were trying to reach the border. The truck dropped us off at an elementary school building. We were ushered into a classroom by a nice, elderly man. I noticed that everybody gave him some money. He brought us some food and told us that he would be back to pick us up at 4:30 in the morning. We were not allowed to turn lights on and were told to be very quiet. Everyone slept on the hardwood floor, and it was very cold. My father wrapped me up in his leather coat and I fell asleep right away.

I still believed we were there to buy food and supplies. I thought we were paying off this man to make sure that he kept quiet so we wouldn't have to share our food supplies with other people.

The morning came quickly and we were on another truck, with

a driver who looked like a young farmer. After a few hours of driving we stopped next to a dense forest. The driver handed maps to some of the men and wished us good luck. I remember his words: "This is as far as I can take you, folks. God bless you and good luck." I saw some of the men give money to the driver, and then he drove off.

I was one of the youngest of the group, with the exception of a set of infant twins. The men discussed the map for a few minutes, and then we started walking. Being November, it was cold and damp, but thankfully it wasn't snowing and we had good visibility. We were told to stay low and try to avoid any clearings, where we would be visible to the border patrols. Crossing the railroad tracks we had to crawl on all fours so we wouldn't be detected by either the Soviet army or the Hungarian guards. We had to go through several wooded areas with very thick brush. My dad was carrying a backpack and a small suitcase. My job was to push the branches out of the way to clear a path so we could keep moving. My hands and arms were bleeding from the thorns and the thick brush, but we couldn't stop because it was going to get dark early and everyone seemed eager to reach our destination while it was still light outside. I began to wonder what the real purpose of this dangerous adventure was, but I was afraid to ask any questions.

We ran out of water by noon, and everyone became increasingly thirsty as the day wore on. At one point our group got separated as we crossed over railroad tracks. As I recall, some of the men thought that thirty people walking in one group would be too conspicuous. They decided we needed to be very careful and so we split into two groups. The family with twins got separated from each other—one baby and his dad were with us, and the other and his mother were with the other group. The mood was somber, and people were very quiet. My instincts told me not to ask any questions and to simply keep walking.

It was getting late and we couldn't go any farther without water. One of the men in our group found a nearby cooperative farm on the map, and it was decided that we needed to take our chances and head there. The water well at this farm was in an open courtyard, which was risky because we could have been quite visible to anyone who was watching from a higher elevation. We had to leave the safety of the forest to get to the well. At this point everyone was so thirsty and so exhausted that nobody cared about anything other than getting water to drink.

Thankfully, the other half of our group was also looking for water and had hiked to the same farm. We met them at the well, and we all filled our containers. It was a joyful moment when the family with the twins reunited, but there wasn't a lot of time for celebration. According to my father, we still had a long way to go. By this time we had covered more than thirty-five kilometers (about twenty miles) on foot that day without stopping to rest. I heard one of the men saying that we just had to get through a cornfield ahead of us, and then cross a very small and shallow lake, and we would be at the Austrian border.

This was when I realized we were not going to buy food but were actually leaving the country, and it scared me. I didn't want to leave my mother, my grandparents, my best friend, and everything that was familiar to me. And I knew that leaving would mean my mother and father would never have a chance to make up and be together again.

I burst into tears and kept telling my father that I wanted to go back home. How could I leave Hungary when I hadn't said goodbye to Mom, Grandma, and Bea? I also had a poem that my mother had written for my grandma's upcoming birthday that I needed to memorize by the time we got back home! But there was no time for any more tears. We had to keep moving. It was late in the afternoon and getting dark again. I was brokenhearted and so confused, wondering about what else might happen.

When we came to the cornfield we saw that the stalks were dry and tall at that time of year, so we felt safe because we were sure that nobody could spot us. We had barely started out into the field when, unexpectedly, we heard gunfire all around us. I know we were all thinking the same thing—that if we got captured, we would be killed on the spot. According to the rumors we heard, the Russian soldiers shot everybody who tried to leave the country illegally. We stopped and tried to stay very quiet.

Then we heard a Hungarian soldier yelling, "Both arms up above your head!" We all put them up. Of course, my father had only one arm, and we heard this voice yell again: "Both arms up or I'll shoot!" That is when I cried out, "My dad has only one arm!" Finally the shooting stopped and we were told to come out of the field and line up so they could check our bags, identify us, and make sure we were unarmed. There were three soldiers, fully armed, and they lined us up. For a moment I thought they were going to kill us. I remembered the war movies I had seen where they would line people up and shoot them dead on the spot.

They checked all our bags and searched us for weapons. Then they started firing their guns up in the air. I thought at first they were practicing before they would turn the guns on us. I stood in front of my dad thinking that if they shot us, the bullets would hit me first and then my dad; that way we could die together. I would not be left alone. Being left alone was always a nagging fear in my heart.

As it turned out, the soldiers were shooting up in the air to signal to the jail a few kilometers from where we had been captured. They were alerting the jail guards to our arrival. It was getting dark and we had to walk another hour to the county jail in Szombathely. We were in the very northern part of Hungary, close to the Austrian border.

It was completely dark by the time we got to the jail. At first all thirty of us were put into a very small waiting room. After a while they started calling people out one by one, and they separated the men from the women. I found out that the men were questioned and if the guards didn't like their answers, they were beaten with rubber hoses. We could hear the men cry out when the guards hit them. The women were left alone and were not questioned at all. I knew in that moment that I wanted to save my father from any kind of beating, no matter what I had to do!

When my father's name was called, I made sure that I sat by the door and put my foot out to keep the door from closing all the way. I wanted to hear what they were asking him. The lieutenant who was checking Dad's identification recognized him and asked, "Mr. Kalman, you are a much admired teacher and conductor in our country. Why would you want to leave your homeland?" Dad's answer was very simple: "I lost everyone and everything that was dear to me during the war. I lost my arm while escaping from a labor camp and my dreams of ever becoming a concert cellist are over. What is left for me here? There is nothing but horrible and painful memories." The lieutenant said, "I understand, but I'm sorry; you have to go into the other room for further questioning." That's when I opened the door, ran to my dad, and hung on to him for dear life. I was not going to let them separate us. I just kept crying and screaming as loudly as I could, "You can't hurt my dad! Hasn't he suffered enough already?" I can't remember what else I may have said, but whatever it was, it worked. I could see the lieutenant's face softening, and finally he said, "I guess you can be considered handicapped. You have suffered enough already. You may go back to the waiting room."

It was a long while before I finally calmed down. Dad and I just sat together, and he kept stroking my head. I was very proud of myself that I could actually do something that would show him how much I loved him!

By the time they finished with our group it was late, and we were all taken to a jail cell. It was a small rectangular room where there were rows of straw mattresses on the floor. Somehow they were able to cram all thirty of us in there. We were so tired that no one seemed to care. At one point they brought us some food, a rice mixture with tomato sauce. It was very dry, but we were so hungry that nobody complained. We ate in complete silence.

There was a guard standing outside the door around the clock. If we had to go to the bathroom, we knocked and spoke through a tiny window. The guard would follow us to the bathroom, wait outside, and then follow us back to our cell.

We were locked up for three days with no news from the outside world. I spent my time memorizing the poem my mother had written for Grandma's birthday. I kept reciting it to pass the time. I tried to befriend our guard and asked him if he would like to hear the poem. I did that every time I went to the bathroom. As I look back on this now, I doubt this guard was even twenty years old; but to me he seemed really grown up.

Then we were released. We were told to go back home and not even to look toward the border if we wanted to stay alive. As it turned out, the jail was getting overcrowded as they captured more and more escapees.

Now, we all needed to find a way to get home. Our group dispersed, and then there were five of us traveling together back to Budapest after Dad found a milk truck that was going to the city. The driver told us the trip would be very dangerous because there were checkpoints in every county. We would need to make ourselves invisible. The aluminum milk cans in the back of the truck were very tall and wide, and on the driver's instructions we hid behind them when we went through the checkpoints. The top of the truck was covered with canvas, which made the back of the truck very dark and helped us be less visible.

As we approached each county the driver would call out, "Checkpoint!" so we would know to hold our breath and not move or make a sound. I have never prayed so hard. The guards had flashlights and scanned the truck very carefully. It was one of the most frightening trips of my life. I was more scared this time than during our entire ordeal. In jail we had been told that we were fortunate to have been captured by the Hungarian guards. They told us the Russians simply shot people dead when they were captured and often raped the women.

Before we even made it home we learned that the revolution had been lost. When we arrived in Budapest that evening, the church bells were ringing. It was 7:00 p.m. and the beginning of the evening curfew. The Freedom Bridge was barricaded with Soviet tanks. The driver told us that because of the curfew we might not be allowed to cross the bridge. My father encouraged me to use my elementary Russian and greet the soldiers, so when we walked toward the barricades I smiled and saluted them as I had been taught in school. They just smiled and waved us through. We must have been quite a sight, having been gone a whole week without bathing or changing clothes. I wasn't feeling very well, and the thorn scratches on my hands and arms had become infected. But by this point I wasn't afraid of much of anything. We had already been through so much, and what could they do to a one-armed man and a little girl? We were allowed to pass without any incident.

We crossed the bridge, and I could barely recognize the city. There were overturned streetcars and buses everywhere. There were dead bodies on the streets and sidewalks, the Hungarians covered with Hungarian flags and the Soviet soldiers with Soviet flags.

I remember thinking that the soldiers looked like young boys who should have been home with their families. I started to cry when I saw all the destruction and the dead bodies. Dad tried to cover my eyes with his knitted shawl so I wouldn't see any more of the horror. I was hugging him so hard he could barely walk. I had the chills and was feeling increasingly sick as we walked to my mother's place. By this time I was coughing a lot, in addition to the infected cuts on my hands and arms. Eventually we made our way home. Grandma and Grandpa were there alone.

Grandma ran over and held me tightly. She hugged my father also. She kept saying over and over, "Thank God you are alive!" She said a thank-you prayer and gave us something to eat. She told us that Mom had gone to my uncle Imre's place to borrow a suitcase and was getting ready to leave to find us. It seemed to me that they had already known Dad and I were not going to the country to buy meat but were actually leaving the country. Dad didn't stay with us very long. He said good-bye and promised he would come and check on me the following week. When I hugged my dad good-bye, I just held on to him for a long time. He looked at me and said, "Be a good girl. I will see you soon." Then he left.

Mom got home shortly after, and we had a very emotional reunion. After that everything went black. I passed out from hunger, exhaustion, and illness. I was very sick. I vaguely remember a doctor standing by my bedside. I also remember Mom and Grandma sitting by the side of my bed trying to remove all the thorns from my hands and arms and putting damp washcloths on my forehead. I found out later on that I had double pneumonia and a severe case of the flu, in addition to the infections. I was in and out of consciousness for a couple of weeks. The most significant memories I have of those two weeks were two very clear dreams, which have remained as vivid in my memory as if they occurred yesterday. At the time, I had the distinct feeling that God was trying to tell me something in both dreams.

The first dream took place in one of the schools where my father was teaching. Everything around me was brown—the walls, the railing around the spiral staircases, and the clothes the kids were wearing. I was on the third floor when the school bell rang, and I was running out of the classroom to find my father. Around me were hundreds of kids, all wearing brown uniforms and running down the stairs. I looked over the railing and saw my father below, being swept away in the rush of the crowd of students trying to leave the school building. I tried to yell for my dad, but I had no voice. I was trying to run after him, but my legs would not move. The harder I tried to run after him, the bigger the crowd became, and eventually I got swallowed up by the sheer number of bodies around me. I woke up sobbing with a very heavy feeling in my heart.

In the second dream, everything was white. I was standing by the window watching a snowstorm outside. It was a huge blizzard, and the wind was blowing furiously. The fierce wind was picking up people like feathers and carrying them through the air. Suddenly I saw my father flying by, and I broke through the glass window with my bare hands. I was desperately trying to grab him and pull him inside. I was so close to touching him but just couldn't quite reach him, and then he was gone.

When I woke up, I had the same heavy feeling as I had felt after my first dream. I stared at my hands for a long time, but there was not a scratch on them and the windows were not broken. As I was telling my grandmother about this dream, somehow I knew that my father had already left Hungary.

A few weeks passed before we could go outside for short periods. One day I asked my mother if we could visit Dad and take him some food. When we did, he wasn't there. The neighbors hadn't seen him in weeks. I knew better. After my two dreams I was sure he was already in America.

The Revolution of 1956: Hungarians celebrate the destruction of
Soviet symbols. Here a statue of Stalin falls.

For a time, Hungarian citizens seize Soviet tanks in the streets of Budapest.

Soviet tanks are rendered useless by Hungarian citizens in the city of Budapest.

Soviet machines of occupation are destroyed.

Hungarians boldly claiming their desire for independence from the Soviets.

Chapter 6
THE OCCUPATION

The Soviet occupation of Hungary began at the end of World War II and lasted nearly forty-five years. During that time, and especially in the early years, the Soviet secret police, the KGB, set about purging occupied territories of political dissidents. It is estimated that some 350,000 Hungarian officials and intellectuals were either executed or imprisoned between the end of the war and the revolution in 1956. Twenty thousand Hungarians died during the revolution, and afterward more than twenty thousand were imprisoned by the Soviets.

Among them was my uncle Imre, my mother's younger brother, who was a well-known poet at the time. He was studying at the University of Budapest, working on his doctorate in literature. He got involved with the organizers of the revolt and passionately believed in the cause. Unfortunately his involvement landed him in jail along with thousands of other brave young men and women. Even the youngest boy in the family, Uncle Bela, showed his support for the freedom fighters and joined with Imre. We prayed constantly that they wouldn't be killed.

During the weeks of fighting we spent a great deal of time in the basement, and everyone was always talking politics. Everyone had a different theory about what was going to happen to our country. People listened to Radio Free Europe, and the Hungarian revolutionaries sent messages to America asking for help, to no avail.

I became a bit of a celebrity to the people in our building, having survived the escape attempt with my father. Everyone wanted to hear all about our journey in great detail. They heard parts of it from my grandparents and my mother, but I guess it was more interesting to hear it from a child's point of view. They probably knew I would tell the true story.

We were also well known in the building because my grandma

fed many people with the supplies she had stored away. She bought more than a hundred kilograms of potatoes that she kept in our storage section in the basement. She stored away foods that would keep for a long time. We had potatoes, rice, beans, flour, sugar, salt, yeast, and a reserve of firewood. Every summer she also would can available fruit and vegetables so we could have jams and compote.

In addition to my Jewish and Christian upbringing, I was deeply influenced by my grandmother's spiritual gifts, which had first emerged when she had suddenly left her home decades earlier and found herself in the circle of people who were waiting for someone to be sent to them. I can say with the deepest conviction that my grandmother wasn't a fake medium in any sense of the word. I myself sat through several séances with her, and the sermons that came through her were quite extraordinary. Since Grandmother only had an eighth-grade education it would have been impossible for her to use the kind of words and expressions she spoke while in a trance. Some of the people speaking through her used such sophisticated vocabularies that my grandfather quite often had to use the dictionary later to understand some of the words she had spoken.

I was told later by others that she sometimes spoke in foreign languages during some of the séances, though she only spoke Hungarian. Her voice was often different during the séances, too, and we could always tell if we had a female or a male speaker communicating through her.

Soon after Grandma and Grandpa came to live with my mother, we received a warning at one of the séances imploring us to start collecting food in preparation for dangerous days ahead. Grandma went to the market and started storing food in our basement, so that if something did happen we would be prepared. Three months later, the revolution broke out, and indeed she fed many of the people in our building with boiled potatoes, rice, and beans from these stored supplies. Perhaps one of my most profound experiences came when I was spoken to by a female spirit, called Elizabeth, assuring me that I would be crossing borders and would join my father. At the time all I knew was that my father had left Hungary; I didn't know where he was at the time. This knowledge definitely helped me not to give up hope when I began my application process to immigrate to the United States and join my father. Ultimately it took seven years.

Grandma was a good Christian woman with the biggest heart known to mankind. She shared our food with the whole building, and was always talking about how Jesus was able to feed multitudes of people. I remember watching her handing out one potato each day to everyone in our building until we ran out. The people were very grateful and loved my little grandma. We boiled the potatoes in the basement in a big pot and ate them like they were the most wonderful delicacy in the world. I would take my one potato, cut circular slices, and then put a little salt and pepper on top. I ate very slowly to make the meal last as long as I possibly could. (Even today that's how I eat baked potatoes.) I would sit with the other kids in the basement and we would have our own little "dinner party," talking politics as if we knew what we were talking about. These were somewhat special times for me because I was just one of the kids in the building and not "the kid from the Jewish orphanage."

One time we had some people visiting from the village where Grandma and Grandpa used to live, and they asked my grandmother for spiritual guidance. After some prayer, Grandmother closed her eyes and a spirit began to speak through her. This spirit asked one of the visitors to stand up, empty his pockets, and ask for forgiveness from his family. Well, the guy who was being addressed by name fell on his knees in tears and took out two flasks of alcohol from his pockets. He was crying like a child. None of us knew that he was an alcoholic who abused his family!

Because Grandmother refused to accept anything from anybody, people would send her anonymous gifts of food or other thoughtful items. It seemed to me that these gifts of food would always come when she and Grandfather needed help the most. God looked out for Grandma always, and it was His grace and the love of Jesus that carried her through her difficult life.

Grandma was a little woman, but her physical strength defied logic. She completely took care of my grandfather for the last twenty years of his life. After a stroke he was paralyzed from his waist down, but Grandmother somehow was able to lift him out of bed. She bathed him, dressed him, and cooked for him—and she never complained about it. She loved her children unconditionally, and she always believed in me, loved me, prayed for me, and was there for me during my loneliest times. I am not sure how I would have coped without her, especially after my father left Hungary. She was truly my main source of support.

She never said good-bye to me without tracing the sign of the cross on my forehead with her fingers for protection. I also continue to do that for my husband and children to this day. When I wanted to take a bite of food from her plate, she wanted to give me her entire plate; I tend to do the same thing for my family. When her family needed her, she dropped everything for them without any questions. I have always tried to live by her example.

One early morning we were just waking up in our apartment when we heard three Soviet tanks coming down on our street. The Technical University was directly across the street from our building, and the Hungarian radio station was only two blocks away. We knew the university buildings were major targets because many of the students were fighting the Soviets, and we figured they would also want to attack the Magyar Radio building to cut off their communications with the public and the outside world.

Our whole building was shaking from the intense vibrations caused by the heavy tanks as they moved down the street toward us. Mom ran toward the window that opened onto the street side of the building, trying to lock the window shutters, but she couldn't quite make it in time. We jumped out of bed quickly, and Grandma and I lifted Grandpa out of bed and dragged him out of the bedroom. We lived on the second level of the building, and we knew that the tanks were tall enough to see inside our room. These tanks had the power to destroy our entire apartment if they fired into it. Mom quickly closed the double doors with panes of frosted glass that led to the kitchen. We dragged Grandpa all the way into the kitchen and put him in the corner by the pantry. I think it deeply hurt his pride that he had to be taken care of when he wanted to be the one protecting his family. If we'd had enough warning of the attack we would have had time to find help to carry Grandpa down to the basement, but it was too late for that now. The tanks were right in front of our building within minutes.

We hid on the floor of the kitchen, in was the farthest spot from the front window. The tank was now right outside the window. The pressure and powerful vibrations from the tank shattered the window glass, which scattered all over the bedroom floor and threw open the unlocked wooden shutters. The sudden motion of the shutters attracted the attention of the tank crew. The bottom pane of glass in the double doors to the kitchen had also cracked, and the hole was big enough to see through. Since I was the smallest, I crawled on all fours to the hole to see what the tank might do next. I watched a Soviet soldier open the upper tank hatch to scan our bedroom for any sign of life, and then turn the turret's gun barrel directly toward the now-open window of our apartment.

I thought for sure that the end was coming. We all held our breath except my grandmother, who was praying in a loud whisper asking Jesus to come to our rescue. My grandfather was very quiet, with tears running down his face. The gun pointed into our bedroom for what it seemed like eternity. Then the soldier turned the gun around and started shooting at the university building. This went on for about half an hour, and then the tank abruptly left, heading toward the radio station with the two other tanks following.

We sat there on the kitchen floor for the longest time, just holding one another. For my grandmother and grandfather, war was nothing new. They had already survived World War I and World War II. They had seen so much war, death, and tragedy that they were ready to accept whatever God had planned for them.

A few days later we heard that the bakery a couple of blocks from us had reopened and we might be able to buy some bread. I was excited to go outside, and I didn't want Grandma to go by herself. We walked to the bakery together and saw a long line of people winding around the corner. It seemed like a peaceful morning.

People were talking quietly among themselves, sharing stories of survival as we all stood in line. All of a sudden gunshots were fired into the crowd. Five people fell out of the line and died instantly. It was such a shocking and surreal scene. People calmly lifted the lifeless bodies and moved them over to the other side of the street. They found Hungarian flags and covered the bodies. Then they came back and continued to stand in line in the hope they might still buy some bread. My grandmother tried to cover my face under her jacket, but at this point I felt numb. I remember saying a prayer of thanks that my grandmother hadn't been shot.

A few days after that, Grandma and I went for a little walk just to get some fresh air, and we saw people looting shops and grocery stores. I was so hungry, I kept asking Grandma if we could go into those shops and get some food, too. If looks could kill! I remember she took my face in her hand and looked at me with her piercing blue eyes. She said sternly, "We will starve to death before we take anything we didn't pay for or work for! The Lord will always provide everything we need." Her intense look and her words left such a powerful impression on me that to this day I would probably starve to death before taking anything from anyone that I didn't earn honestly.

Once we were told that we would be getting some care packages from America. Everyone was very excited over such wonderful news, but nothing happened for a few weeks. Then one day there were several trucks on the streets and some of our Hungarian soldiers were handing out toothpaste, toothbrushes, gum, candies, and chocolates. It was like getting Christmas presents in January. This was the first time I got to experience the generosity of the American people firsthand.

In 1957, after the revolution ended, my grandparents couldn't continue to stay with mother any longer because there were constant quarrels regarding her lifestyle, and Mom asked them to leave. It broke my heart. They couldn't afford much, so they rented a single room in a house from a very nice couple in one of the suburbs called Pesthidegkut. This small room was such a special haven for me where I spent most of my time when school was out. There were two beds against the wall, one for Grandpa and the other for Grandma and me. The bed was not wide enough for two people side by side. The only way we fitted was by sleeping at opposite ends. A wood-burning stove was on one side of the room, and next to it was a very small table where Grandma prepared all the meals. There was a dining room table in the middle of the room that somehow fitted the whole family when they came home for holiday meals. There was a special armchair by the window for my grandfather; there he spent most of his days sitting and reading and sometimes looking out the window, which faced the garden. On one side of his chair was a big bookcase full of books—mostly historical fiction and biography. On the other side was a small end table where he kept his pipe and some more books, as well as a small radio. In the evenings we listened to it for the news and theatrical presentations. Next to the bookcase was an old china cabinet with all the dishes and some storage space on the bottom. Across the room was a clothes closet where Grandma also kept the Danish doll that my father gave me. I always knew she was safe there.

There was no running water inside, so we had to go outside and fill buckets from the well several times a day. There was no bathroom indoors, so we had to go to the outhouse when nature called. The nights were always the worst because I was too scared to go outside to the bathroom by myself. Grandmother always got up and came with me, holding a candle so I could see where I was going. She always waited for me outside, rain or shine. We bathed in a small tub that Grandma kept under our bed. We had to heat the water on the stove to be able to wash ourselves in warm water.

At night my feet would get so cold that Grandma used to put a pair of warm socks on my feet and then blow on them to warm them with her breath. Many years later I did the same thing for my children, as I recalled how my grandmother was trying to keep me warm. She always made me feel special, and she never failed to tell me that no matter how bad things were, God loved me and had great plans for my life. I desperately wanted to believe her.

A seemingly endless parade of Soviet tanks enters the city.

During the Soviet Occupation, travel through the city was restricted at every point. The tanks were everywhere.

Chapter 7
HARD YEARS

E ventually the fighting wound down. The shelling and the shooting stopped, and life slowly returned to the way it was before. The Communist government was reestablished and both of my uncles, along with hundreds of other university students, were eventually let out of prison.

Mom enrolled me in a school near our neighborhood, and for a brief moment I believed that she would actually want to be my mother and care for me. She often said that when my father was trying to take me away from her during our attempt to leave Hungary, she could not bear the thought of losing me. Her maternal feelings, however, were short-lived, especially after my grandparents moved out of her apartment. Mom resumed her old dating habits, and men were coming in and out of her life just like before. As time went on it became clear to me that nothing had really changed, and I would be better off going back to the orphanage.

I spent a lot time by myself in those days. Mom was working in a bookstore during the day, but I never knew where she was in the evenings. Sometimes I got so worried that I would roam the streets the way I had before, trying to find her. I was familiar with the cafés, bars, and restaurants she would frequent, so I would look for her in those places. I would pray to God to make me invisible so people in the bars wouldn't hurt me. The truth is that nobody ever bothered me; as if I had a protective shield around me. In fact, even though they were intoxicated, some of the people tried to help me look for my mother. By this time and after the revolution and our attempted escape, I felt more grown-up and different from the other kids around me.

If it was a cold night and I didn't have a key, the building manager and his wife (who must have felt sorry for me) would invite me to come and sit in their kitchen by the stove until Mom came home. Sometimes they gave me hot chocolate or tea and kept me company. Eventually, Mom would come home, but most of the time she would have a male companion with her.

Mom always had a problem with managing money. The minute she had any, she spent all of it. When she ran out she would sell some of her clothes or furniture. She was a regular customer at the pawnbroker's shop. One day I went home to pick up my cello, and it was nowhere to be found. When I questioned my mother she told me that someone had broken into her place and stolen my cello. Interestingly, there was nothing else taken from the apartment, only my cello. I was devastated, and I knew that she had probably sold it because she needed cash. When I said as much, she denied it and spanked me for calling her a liar. This was one of the really low points in our relationship. I was brokenhearted over this incident for a very long time.

I finally heard from my father, receiving a long letter on April 24, 1957. It was my tenth birthday. He was in New Jersey, staying with his cousin Sylvia. She and her family had immigrated to America when World War II broke out and the persecution of the Jewish people began. In those days most of the mail was censored, so Dad couldn't say much about how he left Hungary. He just said that he was very sorry he left the country without me, but he didn't want to put me in danger again. He promised that he would try to take care of me regardless of the distance between us. He said he had already made arrangements for my return to the orphanage, and for me to continue my cello lessons with one of his musician colleagues, "Uncle" Paul. In closing, he said that he wanted me to come to America so I could have the opportunity to go to university, get a good education, and have a better life. He wanted me to be with him, and that gave me some hope and I was happy.

I received letters from my father regularly, about once a month. All the letters went to Uncle Paul, and he gave them to me when I went for my weekly cello lessons. In those letters my father made it clear that I had no future in Hungary. There were many reasons for this. First, as a descendant of a once-wealthy Jewish family I would not be allowed to attend the university in Budapest, or anywhere else in the country, under the Communist government. I would have to have been from the working class to qualify. The fact that my father had defected would make it even harder for me to be accepted. Also, he was justifiably concerned about the unstable political climate in Eastern Europe. He knew it wasn't safe for me.

I am certain he was also concerned about my mother's lifestyle. He knew well that she had lost everything he had left her, and that her second marriage had ended as well. When I told him my cello was lost, he made arrangements for me to use another one with the help of Uncle Paul. I'm sure my father knew my cello had probably been sold because Mom needed cash. The new cello didn't sound the same, and no matter how much I practiced I couldn't find the richness of the sound from my first cello. It just was never as special to me as the first one had been. Still, Uncle Paul was a wonderful teacher, and I looked forward to my weekly lessons. Being at his place made me feel more connected to my father.

Dad had a plan to bring me to America, and I applied for my passport to leave the country almost immediately after hearing from him in 1957. It took about six months to hear back from the ministry each time I applied. When it was refused, I was allowed to appeal, and then I had to wait another six months before I could apply again. Uncle Paul was very kind and helped me navigate the red tape. He supported me every step of the way with the application process and was always very encouraging when I kept getting turned down. While I kept hoping for a miracle—that my mother would change and become more responsible—I knew in my heart that someday I would leave Hungary.

My best friend Bea and her mom were also applying to immigrate to America, where she had many relatives. We promised each other that no matter what happened, we would always be friends. We vowed that even if one of us got out of Hungary and the other had to stay, we would still keep in touch and continue to help each other.

I always knew my future was in America with my father. But I also had to face the fact that there was no way of knowing when, or even if, that would happen. I still needed to work toward a future in Hungary. I immersed myself in my studies and decided to do everything to succeed in school and get high marks in the youth Communist Party, too. I continued to play cello and to participate in the orphanage fund-raisers. I was involved in any community activity that would earn me extra points and bring recognition to me as a top student, both academically and in civic activities. I sang in the youth Communist chorus and participated in all the parades, carrying our flag and wearing my ever-present red neckerchief.

I read all about Marx and Lenin and began to believe that they were good men. I believed that equality was a good thing. If I had a bowl of soup, everyone should be able to have the same bowl of soup as I had. I believed that the government should take care of everyone. Little did I know at the time that "equality" under the Communist system didn't actually mean equal opportunity for everyone. Members of the Communist Party were the upper class. They had the luxury cars, the weekend homes, and the high salaries. We were told this was a good thing because they were taking care of the people.

The very idea of America was confusing for me. I heard about the great wealth that people enjoyed there, but I was also told that America was an imperialist state taking over other countries and forcing people to follow the American way of life. Until I came to America I had no idea that there was a strong middle class with a higher standard of living than many of the wealthiest people enjoyed in Hungary. Nobody told us about all the great things America had to offer, such as freedom of the press, freedom of choice, freedom of religion, and the opportunity to become anything you wanted to be if you worked hard. Still, I knew in my heart there had to be good reasons why America was the place where so many people wanted to live. I wondered what was so special about America that thousands of people would leave Hungary during the revolution for her distant shores. So often they left everything they owned behind, including their close family members.

When I was in eighth grade I was put in charge of the first- and second-grade girls in the orphanage. At age fourteen I became like their surrogate mom. I had to check their homework and make sure they were clean and ready for school every day. At night I read them stories (or I just made up stories) when I tucked them in for bed. I sat on a different bed each night, and when I finished my story I would give everyone a hug and a kiss. I still remember the feeling in my heart when I felt those children's arms around my neck. I think I needed those hugs more than they did! After a while they started calling me "Mommy," and I loved it. I used to have nightmares that I would be a terrible mom because I didn't have a good example to follow. Having the experience with these precious children put my mind at ease. I knew that I would be a good mother someday if God gave me that special privilege.

Another special aspect was that every year the Center of the Jewish Synagogue planned a couple of big fund-raisers to support the orphanage and to raise money for food, clothing, and books for the children. For reasons unknown to me, I was selected to go to these fund-raisers and perform at the opening ceremony. I would hand out beautiful bouquets of flowers to each participating artist.

Aunt Olga wrote poems that I would perform as part of the opening ceremony. The night before each event, she would give me a poem and then lock me in her bathroom so I wouldn't have any distractions while I memorized the lines. If the poem was too long and if I wasn't memorizing fast enough, she made me get on my knees on the stone floor so I would be motivated to learn faster. The floor was always so cold that I could barely feel my knees. Not surprisingly, I became really good at memorizing those poems very quickly! For my reward, Aunt Olga would give me a piece of candy from her special candy bowl.

I forgot all about the cold bathroom floor when I briefly got to share the stage with many famous artists. When I handed them the flowers after their performances, they always gave me a big hug in return. It was truly an extraordinary experience to share time backstage with all those famous people I used to read about in magazines. They were always very kind to me.

During those years I excelled in almost everything. Academically, I was at the top of my class; I was doing quite well with the cello; and I earned high marks in the Youth Communist Party, as I prepared myself to be successful in Hungary in case I wouldn't be able to immigrate to America. My life at the orphanage was relatively stable, but summers were a different story.

When school would let out for the summer recess, I had a couple of choices. I could be sent to a Jewish foster home like most of the rest of the kids or go to my grandparents' place. I opted for the latter. In my ten years I had to go a foster home only once after my father left Hungary. I stayed with a very nice Jewish family that had two girls about my age who were both friendly to me. Toward the end of my stay with them, my mother surprised me with a visit. I was thrilled to see her, but later I found out that she slept with the father of this family while she was there. I was so embarrassed to learn this and I hoped that I would never have to face those kind people ever again.

I knew my grandparents had very little money because Grandpa's pension was minimal, so when I was twelve I got a job in a chocolate factory to help out. I was very excited to be able to make some money and help my grandmother during the summer. I had to get up at 4:00 every morning and take three different streetcars to get to work by 8:00 a.m.

The job wasn't very exciting. I had to scrape spilled chocolate off the floor where the workers were making truffle-like chocolates. I worked until 2:00 p.m., and then it took at least two hours to get back to Grandma's place. I usually just fell into bed early so I could wake up the next morning and start all over again. I often wasn't hungry for supper when I got home because I had already eaten plenty of chocolate at the factory. The summers weren't really vacations for me, but I was happy and proud to be able to make some money and help out my grandparents. I really looked forward to paydays because Grandmother and I would go grocery shopping and buy meat, bread, milk, and butter, as well as special things she normally couldn't afford.

I worked in the factory for two summers, and people generally were very nice to me. I still remember being embarrassed about the calluses on my fingers when I had to go back to school. I was always hiding my hands because all my nails were broken, and I had cracks on my fingers from all the scrubbing. It was especially embarrassing when I had my cello lessons because my hands looked so bad.

Grandmother was very worried about me working so far away from her place, but I didn't mind it at all. Being busy helped me not to think about my mother, who wasn't around much at this time. I wondered where she was. At first my grandparents tried to keep her whereabouts a secret, but after not hearing from her for six months or so I knew something was terribly wrong. As it turned out, she was in prison. She had been convicted of embezzlement!

I found out the details later. When she worked in a bookstore, she was often left by herself to run the shop. At first she just took a few dollars from the register to make ends meet, with the intention of paying it back. Then, when she needed more money, she started taking more cash out of the register. Eventually she got caught.

One Sunday morning, Grandmother told me that I could go with her to visit Mom in prison. Or course, I missed her, but I was afraid to see her in such a place; my brief stay in jail during the revolution was still very much alive in my memory. Actually, the prison where she was locked up was much worse than the jail where I had been.

When we arrived at the prison in Budapest, we were checked in along with a lot of other people. I kept thinking, *Do all these people have family members in prison? What kinds of crime could they have committed?* I was very nervous and just prayed that I wouldn't see anybody from the orphanage. I didn't want anyone to know about this. Everyone always thought that my mother must be sick because she hardly ever came to see me. I made up different stories about her various ailments so people wouldn't think badly of her or me.

We were ushered into a fairly small room, four people at a time. We stood in front of a glass wall with a hole in the middle. The prisoners came out as they were called to meet their visitors. Finally I saw my mother, and I began to shake and cry so hard that I don't know whether I even said anything at first. My grandmother didn't fare too well either, but at least she was able to ask Mom some questions regarding her circumstances and to see whether she needed anything we could provide. Mom said she was okay and just trying to work very hard so they would let her out early for good behavior.

Mom had lost a lot of weight, her hands looked very dry and cracked, and her face was sunburned pretty badly. But to me she was still beautiful. I wanted so desperately to hug her, but all I could do was touch the glass that separated us. I tried my hardest to smile, and told her I loved her before we left. She looked so vulnerable, and this time around we could not do much to help her. She had to serve her time.

The following summer I moved in with my grandparents again and went back to my job at the chocolate factory. One day I was coming home from work and a neighbor stopped me on the way to let me know that a "peasant lady from the country" was visiting my grandparents. I didn't think that we were expecting anybody, so I was curious to see who it could be. I thought it might have been someone who either needed help or came to thank Grandma for help she had given them in the past.

I was not prepared for what happened next. I opened the door to Grandma's place and the first thing I saw was Grandpa sitting in his chair, crying. On the other side of the room, in the corner by the window, Grandma was rubbing lotion on the hands and face of our visitor. She was also crying. As I got closer, I realized that the "peasant lady" was my mother. I barely recognized her.

Mom was very thin. Her skin was dry like paper, and her fingers were black from all the fieldwork at the prison. I was sobbing as I hugged her, and it felt so good to be with her again. We all just cried and talked for hours. For the next few days I had my mother all to myself and I was happy!

There was one gentleman in Mom's life whom I liked, and I was quite sure that he loved her very much. His name was Gyula

Kekesi, and Mom dated him on and off for many years. Ironically, Gyula had been our next-door neighbor at the Vaci Street flat when my mother and father were still married. He was always very kind to me and gave me special treats. He was also the man who called the building manager to break down the door when my parents left me alone the night they had their last big fight years before. Mom always told me that Gyula was a nice man, but not very exciting for her taste. After a few months of dating him, she would break off the relationship and move on to someone else.

There were a few things I really liked about Gyula. He always spoke about my father with great respect and admiration. He treated my mother very well and was always very kind to me. He was a self-made man and was very proud of the fact that even during the darkest days of Communist Hungary, he never worked for the government but always had his own independent business. He invented a special multifunction ruler that was used in all the high schools for geometry. He had been able to acquire a permit to sell his rulers in schools all over the country, and he made a good living. I used to think many years later that he could have become a very wealthy man in America. He was a self-starter and a very hardworking man, full of creative ideas and dreams. How he was able to have his own business under the darkest days of the Communist regime is still a complete mystery to me.

When Mom got out of prison, Gyula was the one who came to her rescue and nursed her back to her old self. When I returned to the orphanage at the end of the summer, I was happy knowing that she was in good hands. I thought she had finally closed the door to her past and all would be well, but after Mom recovered she resumed her nightlife and didn't stay with Gyula. She found a small apartment in the city, started working in a café, and was doing well for a while. Then we made plans to spend a long holiday weekend together. When I got to her place, she was with George, her second ex-husband, once again!

To see her with this man again after everything he had done to her was almost more than I could take. The power he had over my mother was incomprehensible to me. She lost the beautifully furnished home my father had left her, sold all her jewelry, and even sold my cello to support herself and this man's gambling habits. For the first time, I spoke up. I told my mother that she had to make a choice between this man and me. To my great disappointment, she chose him.

It was too late for me to go anywhere else, so I was stuck with them for the night. Mom's place was a one-bedroom apartment. The only place I could go was the kitchen or the small bathroom to get away from them while they were having sex (which made me feel very uncomfortable and almost nauseous). I ended up spending the night sitting on the stone-cold kitchen floor, using a pillow to make it softer and warmer. I put the pillow up against the wall so I could lean back, which was only slightly more comfortable. I was just waiting until daybreak to take the first bus to my grandparents' place. The kitchen floor was so cold that my body felt completely numb when I got up. I cried the entire night, wondering why my mother would rather spend the night with this horrible man than with me. I was certain there was something terribly wrong with me that my mother had no desire to love me at all. In reaction to what I saw with my mother, I resolved during that night never to allow any man to control me and never to marry a man, so that I could control my own destiny at all costs.

Then I did something I had never done before. I took money out of my mother's wallet—just enough for the bus fare. My grandparents lived too far away, otherwise I would have walked. I left a note for Mom saying only this: "You have made your choice! Good-bye and I will pay you back for the bus fare."

I got on the first bus at 6:00 a.m. I saw a young couple on the bus looking very much in love and ignoring everyone around them. As I was watching them I thought to myself, *If love and sex are so powerful that you ignore your own kid and your family, then why would I want any part of it? I would rather be alone for the rest of my life.*

My grandparents were not expecting me, but when Grandma saw me she knew something was wrong. I fell into her arms, sobbing, trying to tell her what had happened. I kept asking Grandma why my parents didn't want me around. What had I done?

Grandmother made me kneel down and pray, and then she said this: "God loves you more than anything in the world, and He has great things planned for you! You must believe in Him and know that He is with you always." She knelt down with me and prayed that one day I would be able to join my father in America. I fell asleep in her arms, exhausted from the night before. Then the most unexpected thing happened. My mother showed up in the afternoon, full of remorse and asking for my forgiveness for what she had done. My grandmother walked up to her, slapped her hard several times, and told her to get out of the house. Even my quiet grandfather spoke up and told my mother to leave! Mom kept saying that she was sorry and just needed to be with me. This time, I said no.

Mom and I didn't see each other for a few months after this incident, but the following January she came to see me at the orphanage. She wanted me to come and stay with her for the weekend. I was apprehensive at first, but she promised me that we would be alone, just the two of us, so I agreed to go. Every time she did come to see me, I was just so happy that I would forget about everything that had happened before. I wanted to be her little girl again— at least for a little while.

She was pretty broke at the time and didn't have much food at home. We were sitting in the kitchen trying to figure out what we could eat, but I didn't care about that. I had my mother all to myself, and that really did make me happy. We went through her cupboards and found some rice, enough for two bowlsful. We boiled it in water, seasoned it with salt and pepper, and served it on pretty plates. It was delicious. We even set the table so we could pretend that we were having a special meal!

After we finished our rice, Mom jokingly said, "After such a nice meal we should have some dessert!" She opened the oven and took out the baking sheets. On them were some crumbs left from her Christmas baking. We scraped all the crumbs onto two little plates and pretended that we were eating some delicious dessert. Mom was a terrific cook and baker, and even those crumbs were good. I can't remember now exactly what we talked about, but I know we laughed a lot.

She suggested that we take a walk to get some exercise and just enjoy the cold but sunny winter day in the city. We must have walked around for a couple of hours in downtown Budapest, looking at displays in different stores and talking about my life at school and my progress with the cello. She knew so little about my life at that point. Then we ran into one of Mom's old boyfriends, "Uncle" Laci. He was a sweet man with a slight limp and a very mild manner. He was on his way to his favorite restaurant for dinner and asked us if we would like to join him. I could tell my mom saw the sudden anxiety on my face, so at first she declined. He was very kind and said that he would just appreciate our company and would take us home in a cab right after dinner. Mom looked at me. I said it would be very nice, so he took us to the famous Astoria Hotel, which had a five-star restaurant. I remember sitting there thinking, *This meal is a far cry from our previous one!* (I think God has a wonderful sense of humor sometimes.) After dinner, Laci took us home in a cab as promised. Mom and I would recall our special "Christmas crumbs" dinner many times, and it remains one of my most special memories from the time I spent with her. It took so little love from my mother to wipe out all my sad memories from the past.

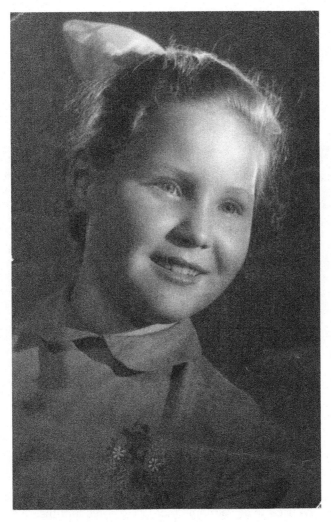

The photo we sent to my father making sure that I
looked happy.

One of the few pictures of Mom and I right after the revolution; when she tried to be "a mom" that lasted three months.

Chapter 8
YOUNG LOVE

It was strange being back at the orphanage, sleeping in my old bed, but at the same time there was a feeling of familiarity, too. I was not a stranger anymore, and everyone seemed to be more accepting of me, especially now that my father was gone.

One of my favorite classes was our weekly religious instruction. I loved the stories from the Old Testament. I thought our teacher, Aunt Margaret, was the most beautiful lady. Her skin was flawless and her eyes were piercing blue. She had the most perfect silver hair, combed as if she just came out of the beauty parlor. Her hands were beautiful, and she had a great story-telling voice.

Each week after our class she would always have a question for us. Sometimes it had to do with what we learned in our class, other times it was a historical or a literary question. Whoever knew the answer won a book of her choice. I really wanted to win, so I read a lot of literature and history and was always up on current events. I did win fairly often, and eventually I ended up collecting quite a library. In high school I had a lot more freedom to pursue my interests and was allowed to join some clubs. I was part of the Shakespeare Club, the Writer's Workshop, the Drama Club, and the Chorus Group. I loved them all.

In my freshman year there was a writing contest. You could write a short story or a poem to enter. The first prize was the equivalent of a hundred-dollar gift certificate for your favorite bookstore. I was pretty excited because I already knew my topic and thought I might have a chance to win something or at least get an honorable mention. I often tried to imagine what it would be like when I finally reunited with my father in America. I knew immediately that my story would be about that dream. The title of my story was, "An Imaginary Meeting with My Father." I wrote the whole narrative in one sitting and after a quick review turned it in, hoping for the best.

Here is the essence of the story as I remember it: In my loneliest moments I used to imagine how and where my first reunion with my father would take place. In my imaginary story I escaped from Hungary by myself, hoping to find my father and surprise him once I got to America. I knew he was alone and needed me to be with him. On the streets of New York I saw my father standing at a bus stop, waiting to get on a bus. It was a very rainy, cold winter day, very much like the day when we tried to escape Hungary in 1956. I recognized his ever-present leather coat and raced toward him, grabbing his arm and saying, "Dad, I found you! I am here! I made it!" He turned around and just stared at me for the longest time, while my tears ran down my face. He was clearly shaken and at first there were no words spoken; but we held on to each other for a long time, trying to take in the moment. He looked older, and I was no longer the nine-year-old little girl he'd left behind. And then we walked and we talked and I asked him all the questions I'd stored up about his past, about his love for my mother and his love for me. Nothing really mattered because we had found each other. My story ended on a hopeful note of forgiveness and love between my parents.

There was a boy at our public high school named Andras Jeles who was very popular; he was also known for writing good poetry. He entered the contest, too, and everyone predicted that he would win because he had won the grand prize two years in a row. He was in his junior year and I was only a freshman. After waiting anxiously for two weeks, we got the results during a school assembly, and I could not believe it when my name was called as the grand prize winner. Andras won the second prize.

There was a special awards ceremony combined with a fundraiser for our school, and the winners were invited to read their work aloud in front of faculty, families, and other invited guests. My mother actually came to this event and sat in the front row. I was very nervous at first, but I got caught up in the emotion of my story and forgot that anyone was even there. When I finished I got a standing ovation (there weren't many dry eyes in the audience).

I could feel Andras' eyes on me as he stood behind the curtain, and my heart skipped a beat.

He congratulated me—the first time we actually exchanged any words. He was larger than life in my eyes, and I never thought a guy like him would ever notice me. He started waiting for me between classes, and often he would walk me back to the orphanage. We talked about everything—our lives, our dreams, the theater, our families, and so on. It seemed to me that he liked me, but I was terrified because my self-esteem was very low. I was a bit overweight and never for a moment thought I was remotely attractive. I couldn't understand what he saw in me; he could have any girl he wanted in our school. Nevertheless, our friendship blossomed and we spent a lot of time together during the summer break.

During this time I was also spending more time with my mother, who was finally living with Gyula. I was happy that he was back in her life, because he was a good man and always very kind to me. It also seemed that Mom was a lot more mature and calm when she was around Gyula. He never made me feel that I was in the way, and it was obvious to me that he really loved my mother and accepted her for who she was. Gyula often told me that I should be at home living with them because I was not an orphan. I told him I couldn't do that unless they were legally married. I knew that would be a big step for him to take; he was a confirmed bachelor and he had never really wanted to marry anyone.

One day, just a few months before my sixteenth birthday, they asked me what I wanted for my birthday gift, and I said I wanted only one thing: for them to make their relationship legal and be married in front of God. I got my wish when they married the weekend before my birthday, and I moved to Gyula's home from the orphanage the following week.

He still lived in the very same apartment on Vaci Street next to the one where my mother, father, and I had lived so many years before. It was a strange feeling to move next door to our old home, yet it was comforting at the same time. I was amazed, and very grateful, that even though Gyula was well aware of my mother's past, he still took a chance on her. He loved her very much.

I told them about Andras, and they were very nice about it. I wasn't sure if I would even see him during our summer break because I was busy working for my aunt Mandi at the Hungarian National Bank, where she was a department head. But Andras did call and invited me to see Shakespeare's *Hamlet* and then took me to a café afterward.

When he came to our apartment to pick me up, I was so nervous that I could hardly breathe! He gave me a shy hug, and I could feel his heart beating really fast (as was mine). In the theater our hands would sometimes touch but I would pull away, not being sure what to do. Being with him alone on a date seemed surreal to me, and I was still wondering how I ended up with the best-looking and most popular guy at our school.

I remember the first time we held hands and he very briefly kissed me. It was pretty obvious that this was the first kiss for me, so he was gentle and almost shy. He made me feel so beautiful. He wrote me sweet love poems and told me that he was in love with me. He knew that I was trying to leave Hungary and immigrate to America to be with my dad, and he did his best to try to talk me out of it. At the time, I kept getting rejected for a visa, so it didn't seem like something that would happen anytime soon. To me, our whole friendship and romance seemed like a dream. Because of him I had many new friends at school, and these were happy times. Our love was pure and innocent and it felt very real.

Of course, Andras wanted more from me that I would physically give him, but he was kind and understanding. The memories of everything I had been through during my childhood took away my desire to discover sexual intimacy. But Andras was almost eighteen, with raging hormones (I was close to my sixteenth birthday, but definitely a late bloomer). One night we were taking a long walk in the moonlight on the shores of the Danube. I guess one could say we started making out. He was kissing me with such passion, at first on the lips then on my neck, and then I felt his hand on my breast. I got a little scared and was trying to take hold of his hand so it wouldn't go below my waist. His emotions were overwhelming, and I almost got caught up in the moment. He told me that he had fallen in love with me, and when he saw from my face that I was scared he apologized for getting so carried away.

We walked back home holding hands, and talked for a long time. I got up my courage and asked him point-blank, "Andras, what was it that made you fall in love with me? All the girls at school are crazy about you, and they are a lot prettier than me. I really want to understand." He looked at me and started laughing. Then he said, "Do you realize I never even looked at your legs? I just saw your face. I saw your eyes. I hear your voice in my dreams and I love everything about you. Ildiko, you cannot explain love."

I was stunned, and when we said good-night he told me again that he loved me and wanted me to reconsider leaving my homeland. For a moment I was tempted to give up my dream of going to America. But I remembered the promise I had made to myself that no man would ever control me or my emotions. Andras' strong feelings scared me, and I didn't think I could love him the same way. I still remember reading the passionate, beautiful, and often sad love poems he wrote for me because he knew that I would eventually leave Hungary. "Romantic love," while it was exciting, was also a frightening mystery to me.

Later that night, at home, I was getting ready for bed and my mother came into the bathroom while I was brushing my teeth. I figured that she wanted to talk to me about my date. Then all hell broke loose. She started hitting me and slapping me in the face and yelling that I was a whore and worse. I really thought she had lost her mind! Then she grabbed me and pushed my face against the mirror and pointed her finger to my neck. There were a couple of red marks on the left side of my neck where Andras had been kissing me. I honestly didn't even know what they were because I didn't feel anything unusual while we were making out.

Gyula came to my rescue and stopped her, but by that time my nose was bleeding and I was a big mess. I looked at my mom and got very angry. The memories of the many men she had slept with in my presence washed over me, and for the first time I addressed the issue. I said, "You of all people! How dare you treat me like this after everything you have done to me? But it's fine because I am going to America to be with Dad. I'll do whatever it takes to get out of here and leave all my horrible memories behind!" She started to cry and kept saying that she just wanted stop me from making the same mistakes she had. We never spoke about that evening again, but I never forgot it. For years afterward, she would try to explain her past, but I didn't want to talk about it. I was afraid I might say something so hurtful that I could never take it back. It was easier, and safer, to say nothing.

My father and I remained in close contact, and all this time I was applying for exit visas to immigrate to the United States. When I got turned down I would appeal, and six months later the process would start all over again. Then, one night, I woke up with a start. I distinctly heard a voice say, "Get up and write a letter to the premier, Janos Kadar, and tell him why you need to leave Hungary and immigrate to America to be with your father." It was a male voice, and it was so real that I got up and looked around to see if anyone was actually there in the room.

I never questioned the voice. I got up, sat down at Gyula's desk, and started writing. It was exactly 2:30 in the morning. I vaguely remember describing the losses my father had suffered during the war. That he had no family in America beside me. That he had only one arm. That he was getting older and needed me to look after him. When I finished the letter I got on my knees and prayed to God and thanked Him for his guidance. Then I just said, "Thy will be done." I mailed the letter the next morning.

Two weeks later, I got home from school and was preparing to start my homework when I heard the mailman dropping letters through the mail slot. I went to the door and immediately noticed a bright yellow postcard from the Ministry of Immigration. In the past all the refusal postcards had been dark pink with bold black letters printed on them. I knew immediately that things were going to be different this time! I started shaking uncontrollably and got on my knees to pick up the postcard from the floor. I closed my eyes and slowly turned it over, praying at the same time. When I opened my eyes, I read, "Please appear at the Ministry of Immigration on Wednesday, 8/23, 1963, at 10:30 a.m."

I was beyond elated. I remember getting on the phone and calling everyone in our family to give them the big news that I might be going to America, but I really don't think anyone believed me. I sent a telegram to my father giving him this wonderful and unexpected news. Then it was time to tell mother and Gyula.

When they got home, I sat them down and said, "Do you remember a couple of weeks ago when I wrote to Premier Kadar to ask permission to immigrate to America? I guess it worked, because this time they didn't refuse my application. I have an appointment next week at the Ministry of Immigration. I think I am finally going to America!"

Gyula was happy for me, but Mom got very upset. She kept saying that God was punishing her for not being a good mother. I think she may have felt guilt for not having been there for me for so many years, and I think she had hoped that by marrying Gyula we could all start over. I tried to reassure her how much God loved her, that He had sent a wonderful man to be by her side, and Gyula would take care of her. I also explained that God had a different plan for me, and I needed to be with my father.

It was very emotional when I told Andras the news. We both cried, and I promised him that we would stay in touch and that if I didn't like America I would come back to Budapest. In my heart I was actually terrified at the idea of leaving everything behind, but I knew there was no turning back.

I was following my destiny.

Chapter 9
LEAVING HUNGARY

My father called me upon receiving my telegram and told me that Uncle Paul would have money for me and coach me on how to get my exit visa quickly. He also told me that the American school year in California would begin on September 16, and he wanted me to start my junior year on time and begin learning the English language immediately.

Then he completely surprised me. He said, "I didn't want to tell you this earlier, but I do need to tell you now. I remarried a couple of years ago, to a good woman named Irma. She knew all about you before I even considered proposing marriage. She is also a Holocaust survivor and a distant relative I met through cousins who left Hungary after the war. She is of Hungarian-Czech descent and speaks fluent Hungarian. You have a half-brother named Robbie. He is almost one year old, and we have another baby on the way. This will take nothing away from you. I want you here with us, and your future is my responsibility. Irma is very much looking forward to meeting you and welcoming you to our family."

I was speechless and really could not process everything I had just heard. The dream of having my father all to myself was gone in an instant. I was really tempted to call the whole thing off and stay in Hungary, but I knew there was no turning back now.

I showed up for my meeting with the ministry at the appointed time. When my name was called, a very stern and unfriendly female secretary ushered me into a large office. I saw a creepy older man sitting behind a large desk looking at some papers. Across the room were a big leather couch and an end table with some newspapers and an ashtray on top. He motioned for me to sit on the couch and then he sat next to me, which seemed a little strange. I recognized my letter to the premier in his hand, and he had a stack of other papers as well.

He started listing all the reasons why I should stay in Hungary. He said that since I had an exceptional school record with many accomplishments, my future in Hungary was bright. I never wavered and told him why my father needed me. I stuck to the contents of my letter, which he obviously had read. I listed all the horrible things that had happened to my father during the war. I reminded him that Dad was getting older now and it was important that I be with him. (Obviously, I was not 100 percent honest with this man, because my father was now a married man with a new family. Thank God they never verified my father's marital status!).

The man was uncomfortably friendly with me and kept taking my hand and putting his arms around me. He sat way too close to me on the couch, and that scared me to death. Nevertheless, I stuck to my script and spoke about the love I had for my father and how much I wanted to be with him. I said I would go even if I had to walk to America on foot. He finally ran out of objections and allowed me to leave. I wondered whether this creepy old man had tried to take advantage of some other young girls before. I was pretty sure he had.

When I came out of the room, I started to shake from nerves. Then I witnessed a miracle. My best friend Bea and her mom were in the waiting room! They were the next appointment after me! We had to pretend that we didn't know each other, but all three of us had tears running down our cheeks as I walked past them. Everything we had talked about and dreamed of for so many years was about to come true. We were excited and apprehensive at the same time. America was a big unknown with so much promise Bea was suffering from a severe case of asthma so she was not able to leave Hungary right away.

She was taken to a sanatorium for treatment for several months. When she got well enough to travel, she and her mom left for New York where they had relatives and planned to live there permanently.

We did stay in touch for awhile and I had a chance to visit her on my way back to Hungary a couple of times. She got married a lot sooner than I did and with our busy lives we lost touch for the next several years.

Right after my meeting I phoned Uncle Paul, and we set a date to meet at his place the next morning. He told me that actually getting my visa could take up to six months, so we would need to pay a few people off in order to expedite the process. He coached me on what to say to the people in the visa office and basically how to bribe them. He handed me a thousand forints (equivalent to a thousand dollars) and told me to not leave the visa office until I had my signed papers in hand. The following day I was at the visa office right when they opened at 8:00 a.m. I showed up in my best school uniform, looking very proper. I was hoping that God would lead me to some nice people who would be willing to help me.

I was ushered into a very dusty old office with a waiting area in front. When I walked in I saw a woman sitting at the front desk, chain-smoking. She asked me what I was doing there. I told her that I needed to get my visa today because I was planning to leave for America in a couple of weeks so I could start my school year on time. She just smiled and told me to sit down and wait until they called my name. I must add that I was the only person there.

After a couple hours of waiting, I walked up to her again and asked her if I could speak with someone so I could get my visa. She took my papers, and I watched as she proceeded to put them in a drawer. She said they would call me in a couple of months. I just stared at her in complete disbelief. Obviously she pretended not to have heard me when I said I needed to get my visa today so I could get to the United States in time to start the school year. I said, as assertively as I could, "How much will it cost me to get my visa today?" She started laughing, but then I took out a hundred-forint bill and said, "I have more money if needed, but I will leave here with my visa today."

She took the money, and then got my visa documents out of the drawer and disappeared into another room. There were three more people who eventually reviewed my papers. It was already noon and I knew that they would close for lunch soon, so I walked up to them again and reminded them that I needed my visa and was ready to pay for it. I must have been such a comical sight—after all, I was only sixteen years old, and in my school uniform and my proper braided hairdo I'm sure I looked like a kid. Finally, I walked up to the front desk, where they were all talking, and put down two hundred forints. I said, "If I could get my visa right now I have this amount of money for each one of you." The looks on their faces were priceless. After that they got to work pretty fast!

The entire process of approving and preparing my visa took less than ten minutes. It basically involved putting three stamps of approval on my passport: one for leaving Hungary, one for my lay-over in Amsterdam, and one for entering the United States through New York. I walked out of that office at 1:00 p.m. with my passport and a visa in my hands.

Next I had to have a meeting with the American ambassador in Buda. I was really looking forward to that because I admired all the impressive buildings there on "embassy row." The area was always beautifully landscaped, with big oak trees providing much-needed shade during the hot and humid months of summer. I used to wonder what the buildings looked like on the inside. The flags of each particular country were proudly displayed at each embassy along with the Hungarian flag. They all had beautiful gardens with flowers blooming everywhere. I thought the American embassy looked the best, but of course I was a little biased.

There was an around-the-clock guard on duty checking papers before anyone could enter the American embassy. After I entered the building, a guard took me upstairs to the ambassador's office on the second floor. He immediately got up from his chair and spoke to me in Hungarian. He welcomed me to America and wanted to know about my family and also my ultimate destination. I told him about my father and that I would be going to the Santa Barbara area where he was teaching music in a high school. He told me that it was a very beautiful place and that I would like it there a lot. He also said I would probably get married after high school, have a family, and live happily ever after. I told him that my dream was to get a university education and that I had no plans for marriage at all. He just smiled at me and wished me good luck.

I was impressed with how polite and kind he was, and I knew that if the American people were anything like this man I would be proud to be an American. The date for my departure was set for Friday, September 13, 1963.

I was certainly one of the lucky ones. Emigration from Soviet-bloc countries had been very difficult since the end of the war, and after the erection of the Berlin Wall in 1961, it became even harder. According to the Council of Europe, only 332,000 Hungarians emigrated to the West between the end of World War II and 1982, and 200,000 more of them had fled during the revolution. This means that at the time I got my visa, the government was clearing only a few hundred Hungarians for immigration per month, an extremely low number compared to the huge numbers of people who wanted out, and even worse than neighboring countries like Czechoslovakia, Romania, Poland, and East Germany, all of whom allowed many more to leave. Hungary was no doubt one of the hardest places to "escape" from, and as a young Jewish girl the odds were definitely against me. I have to believe it was God's plan, and through His grace I was let free.

My mother took my decision to leave Hungary very hard. She was now thirty-four years old and finally married to a decent guy, but the guilt of her past still haunted her. She constantly wanted to talk about the past and explain things to me, but I didn't let her. I was so afraid that all the pain of being neglected for so long would burst out of me and we would end up having a fight. I didn't want to leave like that. I kept reassuring her that the past was past and that I was sure she'd done the best she could. I told her that we needed to make the most of our last couple of weeks and cherish our time together.

The last few weeks before my departure flew by. I said good-bye to Andras, and he was very sweet and wished me well. It was sad, but we promised to stay in touch. The hardest, though, was saying good-bye to my beloved grandmother. She was a widow by this time and in poor health. When Grandfather died they had been married nearly sixty years, and life was hard for her without him. Years of taking care of him had caught up with her, but it had also given her a purpose and kept her going all these years.

Grandma's love for me was unconditional, and I adored her beyond words. She always told me that my place was with my father, and no matter how bad things got, God and Jesus loved me and had wonderful plans for my life. She always said, "Don't ever be afraid, because there is a guardian angel watching over you, and when God takes me home I will be watching over you, too." In addition to her spiritual gifts, she always had a sixth sense about things, and during our visit she kept talking about my father and that I needed to be with him. I was almost sure she knew I was leaving, she just didn't know when.

Packing was very easy. I had one large suitcase with a couple of changes of clothing, and the rest of the contents were gifts for my father and his wife. Dad specifically asked me not to bring much clothing, because the style of dressing was so different in America that I would probably not want to wear any of my things from home. He assured me that as soon as I got there we would go shopping for school clothes and anything else I might need.

My last night at home was very emotional. None of us slept a wink; we just talked all night. My mother and Gyula made me promise that if I was not happy I would tell them the truth and they would arrange for me to come back home. Mom bought me a very nice skirt suit with a pretty blouse for the trip, and I packed some of my favorite Hungarian novels to read during the journey. Basically, I left Hungary with one suitcase and a handbag containing my papers and a few photos of my family. I had some gifts for my father and his wife and a small toy for my little brother.

The process of packing was almost an out-of-body experience. It seemed as if I was just going through the motions but I wasn't really present. My mother would try to help me pack, but we would just start crying. She asked, "Why do you have to go now, when my life is finally on the right track?" My answer was simple: "I'm so happy things are going well in your life. See how wonderful God is? Remember that I'm not leaving you alone, that there is someone who loves you and will take care of you. Now I need to be with my father." She still tried to get me to stay. She said, "But now I can be your mother in a way I couldn't before." I said, "You will always be my mother, and I love you just like I love my father. The fact that I am able to emigrate to America right now is such a miracle that I have to believe I am following my destiny." I was so happy, on the one hand, that Mom actually loved me, but I also remembered the physical ache in my heart I had experienced all those years while I waited for her to say those words.

There is no doubt that I was very torn about leaving Hungary, the country that I knew so well and loved so deeply. And I was certainly a little scared about facing the unknown, but then I would pray and become calm. I knew I was following the path that God had planned for me.

Chapter 10
AMERICA

We left for the airport very early in the morning because we knew the authorities would take a lot of time checking all my immigration papers. I wasn't feeling too well and had an upset stomach from lack of sleep. I was also very nervous because I had never flown before, and I had no idea what to expect. I knew I had a tendency to get motion sickness easily.

Mother and Gyula stayed with me for as long as they were allowed, and then the time came to say our good-byes. Mom was crying so hard that I was afraid she was going to faint. Gyula cried also and told me to be good and write to them often. He always liked and respected my father, and knew I would be well cared for. Mom kept saying, "You are going so far away and you don't know anybody. Who will watch over you?" It was interesting how genuinely worried she was about me at age sixteen, after not being concerned at all when I was a little girl. But it felt really good to see her caring about me.

Then Mom and I embraced, and she held me so tightly I could hardly breathe. Feeling her arms around me was wonderful and it was hard to let go. I knew she did love me after all. She kept saying, "There is still time to change your mind, to stay home and not leave the country that you love so much!" And for a brief moment I was tempted to turn back and just go home. I thought about my father who was married now and had another family. I thought about the great challenge of moving to a country where I didn't even speak the language. I thought about all the terrible things we were taught in school about "imperialist" America.

I also knew that almost everyone in Hungary would gladly take my place and leave everything behind for the opportunity to go to the United States. I remembered Dad's words when he told me I had no future in Hungary. My grandmother, whom I had always trusted, had said that my future was with my father because he was the one who had taken care of me in the past and would take care of me in the future. I broke away from my mother's embrace and with a very heavy heart walked to my plane. America, here I come!

My route was pretty direct. I flew on the Hungarian airline, Malev Airlines, to Amsterdam, and from there on Pan American Airlines to New York, where I had to go through the whole immigration process in America. Then I took the final Pan Am flight to Los Angeles. It was quite a journey.

I managed okay between Budapest and Amsterdam because almost everyone on the plane was Hungarian (there were also a few Russian civilians). The adventure really began on the Pan American plane. It was the biggest plane I had ever seen, and nobody around me spoke a word of Hungarian. A very kind stewardess took all my documents and put me in the very first row. It was obvious that I was scared and had no idea what I was supposed to be doing. Incidentally, all the attendants were tall, slender, and very pretty. They gave me all kinds of little gifts and lots of special chocolates, and I kept thanking them in Hungarian. I saved all the goodies to give to my father and his family.

The flight from Amsterdam to New York was very long, and I got really sick. I kept throwing up and couldn't keep anything down. All the foods, which looked so different to begin with, tasted awful because my stomach was so upset. I did learn a few words, though, like "please," "thank you," "coffee," and "help." Anyway, they showed infinite patience and kept checking on me to make sure I was okay. I was so embarrassed. I found it most amazing that everyone was always smiling at me and just looked so happy. I had not experienced anything like this before.

When we approached JFK I was almost blinded by all the lights of the big city. Then, when we landed in New York, I thought I was on another planet. Customs and Immigration was quite an ordeal. I had never seen automatic doors and escalators, and I was so confused when the doors just opened by themselves (and the escalators looked really scary!). I was sure I would trip or fall. I must have been quite a pitiful sight, as I would run after the automatic doors as they opened or just stand and stare at the escalator, wondering how to get on. Luckily there was always someone who would come to my aid, take me by the arm, and help me to get through the next step. Thank God all my papers were in order, because I didn't have any idea what anyone was talking about in English!

After I got through Immigration, someone walked me onto the next plane for the final leg of my journey. I was just praying that I was on the right plane. There was a nine-hour time difference between Hungary and America, and it seemed as if I had been traveling for two days. Yet with the time difference, I left Hungary on Friday, September 13, and arrived in Los Angeles on the same day at 3:30 in the morning!

As the plane approached Los Angeles I was once again dazzled by all the lights I could see from the air and by the sheer size of the metropolitan area. I thought, *What do people do here with all the lights on all the time? Don't they ever sleep?* I started getting very nervous and excited at the same time. Would my father be waiting for me? Would he like me? Would he be really happy to see me? Would our meeting be anything like the short story I wrote a year earlier? Would he be disappointed when he saw me? Finally the plane landed and the door opened, and when I looked out the window I immediately saw my father standing as close to the tarmac as he was allowed.

They let me off the plane first, and I ran down the stairs into my father's arms. I was crying and didn't want the moment to end. He seemed deeply moved also. The last time he had seen me I was nine years old. Someone came over to us from the plane and handed me my suitcase as we started walking toward Dad's car. As we were walking, Dad looked at my skirt and asked me if I'd had an accident on the plane. I told him that I did get sick while flying, but other than that I was fine. Then Dad said to go to the bathroom and check my skirt. I went into the bathroom and when I turned my skirt around, I saw a number of brown stains. Then I realized what had happened. All the chocolates I was saving for my father and his family had melted all over the back of my skirt! I'll never forget what dad said next. "Welcome to America. In this country you even *sit* in chocolate!"

Dad was extremely proud of America, and he had worked very hard to make a life for himself and his family here. His opportunity to continue making a living from music came through his best friend, Fred Balazs. Their friendship was unique and lasted throughout their lives. Fred was also of Jewish descent, and was a well-known violinist and composer who had played chamber music with my father before the war. He also managed to survive the labor camp, and he had escaped to America as World War II was winding down. Still, he and Dad stayed in contact, and Fred always encouraged Dad to immigrate to America.

When my father finally did escape in 1956, he first went to stay with cousins in New Jersey. Fred was the conductor of the Tucson Symphony, and was married with a family of six children. Dad was eager to reconnect with Fred, and he also wanted to make his own way in America. Staying with relatives in New Jersey was just a temporary solution, and Dad never wanted to be a burden on anybody.

After staying only two weeks with his cousins, Dad traveled to Tucson to meet up with his old friend. The last time they had seen each other had been in 1944 at the labor camp. Fred helped my father find a place to live as well as a job. He also arranged for my father to get a room free of charge from a wealthy elderly woman who was a huge supporter of the Tucson Symphony. In exchange, my father taught her how to play piano. He started giving private lessons to students and teaching piano, violin, and, of course, cello. He saved and purchased a motor scooter to get around, and became an expert motorcyclist—with one arm. Dad went on to earn his master's degree in instrumental music in Tucson so he would be eligible to teach high school. Unfortunately, he was unable to teach college in spite of the fact that he was more than qualified. To be a university professor he would need to play in the orchestra, and of course that was out of the question.

Dad had lived in Tucson for a couple of years when he got an offer to become the music director for Carpinteria High School, where he would oversee the marching band, the school chorus, and the school orchestra. Dad moved to Carpinteria, but stayed in touch with Fred for the rest of his life.

On the two-hour ride from the airport in Los Angeles to Carpinteria (a small town near Santa Barbara), Dad told me about my stepmother, Irma. She was an orphan from age four and was raised with the help of relatives who lived close to the Czech-Hungarian border. She was also a Holocaust survivor, so they shared a lot of history and that was an important part of their relationship. Dad also told me that he had always wanted three children, just like the family he grew up in. Irma had never been married and also had dreams of having a family. Dad was forty-seven when they met, and Irma was in her mid-thirties. The timing was perfect for both of them.

I could tell my father loved his wife but that it wasn't a passionate love. They were looking for the same things in life and were able to fulfill those needs for each other. Irma was well educated, with a master's degree in nutrition, and she worked for the Health Department. They were married in 1961. My brother, Robbie, was born on October 2, 1962.

Dad was very excited for me to meet my little baby brother for the first time. He also kept reassuring me that Irma would be a good friend and a lot of help to me while I adjusted to my new life in America. She knew from the beginning that Dad had been married before and had a child he was planning to bring to America. Dad also explained that the only reason Irma could not come to the airport to welcome me was that she was eight months pregnant with my second little brother. She also wanted my father and me have this special time alone. I appreciated her thoughtfulness very much.

Finally we were home and it was early Saturday morning—about 7:00 a.m. Irma was up waiting for us and gave me a warm welcome. I was beyond exhausted and just wanted to go to sleep. I lay down on a sofa bed that she had ready for me in the family room, and I was out like a light.

I had no idea what time it was when I woke up. The first thing I saw was little Robbie crawling around my bed, curiously trying to figure out who this stranger might be. I was nervous because I wanted my baby brother to like me (and I wanted to make a good impression on my stepmother). Robbie was a beautiful baby, and I was very excited to hold him. When I sat up in bed and reached out to him, he started making funny gurgling sounds and kept saying "Up, up, up," so I picked him up; he and I played for a long time. Of course I was speaking in Hungarian, but Robbie didn't seem to care. We understood each other just fine!

Dad told me that I should try to get some rest because I was enrolled to go to school on Monday. He was preparing me for the challenging times ahead as I would need to get used to a very different way of life and also learn the English language very quickly. We sent a telegram to my mother to let her know I had arrived safely and I would write her soon.

Everything still felt and looked very strange to me. I had spent my entire life in a big city, and the town of Carpinteria looked like a big village to me. I couldn't believe everybody had a car (or two) in the driveway. No one seemed to walk on the streets—they drove everywhere (sometimes even across the street!). Dad told me that in America most people live in the suburbs, with the exception of big cities like New York or Chicago. In the suburbs everyone had a television, dishwasher, washing machine, and dryer. I found out later on that you didn't have to be rich to have all these luxuries. These things were standard in the average American home. My father's home was very modest, but it had everything the family needed. For the first time in my life I had my own little room and my own bathroom with a shower. I had some privacy at last!

In the afternoon my father took me to the supermarket, and that was quite an experience. I was in awe because it was such a big place and people were just helping themselves to whatever they wanted. I was so used to going to different markets for meats, dairy, produce, fruit, and so on. Here, everything was in this one giant place, and you could take a shopping cart and fill it with anything you needed. And nobody told you not to touch things!

I asked if I could have chicken and tomatoes every day, because in Hungary we could eat chicken only on high holidays like Christmas or Easter. Tomatoes were available in Hungary only when they were in season, and they were always expensive. Dad said chicken was the cheapest meat in America and that I could eat all the tomatoes I wanted all year round. The produce section with all the fruits and vegetables looked perfect to me. The first time I saw it, I just stood there for the longest time because I was waiting for someone to measure things out for us. My father was laughing and enjoying every minute of my first American supermarket shopping experience. He handed me a few plastic bags and told me to start picking out what I wanted.

I ran for the tomatoes, grapes, apples, and berries, but every time I picked something out I was looking around in case somebody was upset because I was taking only the most perfect-looking specimens. I asked if it was okay that I didn't take any of the soft tomatoes but just the firm ones. Dad was smiling and said, "Here we throw all the bad produce away." He added, "I was just like you when I was taken to an American supermarket for the first time. I will never get tired of watching immigrants' reactions—especially from Eastern European or Third World countries—when they step into these supermarkets for the first time. It always reminds me all over again how lucky I am to be in America!"

I thought I was in Paradise. Everyone in the market was very kind and smiling at me because it was obvious that I was a "first-timer." Of course, my father was eager to introduce me to people he knew at the market. He was proud to tell them I had just arrived from Hungary. Everyone was so nice, smiling at me and talking to Dad. I smiled back, feeling completely overwhelmed in this new environment. I didn't understand a word anyone was saying to me, and though I smiled back at all of them, when we got home I just burst into tears. How would I ever learn this language quickly? How would I ever feel comfortable with these people who knew nothing about me and with whom I had nothing in common?

On Sunday, Dad suggested we take a walk and see the Pacific Ocean I had read so much about. It was only a couple of blocks

from our house. What an incredible sight it was! It was a far cry
from the Danube or the Tisza or even Lake Balaton; they seemed
no bigger than a bathtub in comparison. Not knowing the power
of the ocean, I ran straight into the water, and a giant wave immediately knocked me off my feet and put me under. I drank a whole
lot of salt water, but Dad was right there to rescue me. After that
experience, to this day I love sitting by the ocean listening to the
waves, but I don't like to go in!

Dad and I walked on the beach for a long time and just talked
and talked. We had so much to catch up on. The first thing I asked
him was, "Why did you leave me without saying good-bye?" He
said, "You were a little girl, and I put you in such danger the first
time I tried to leave. I didn't want that happen to you again." We
talked for a long time. He shared with me the painful experience
of his marriage with my Mom, and made it clear that he preferred
me to have very little contact with her going forward. That hurt
me deeply. I realized later that it was out of fear. He was afraid I
would take the same path as she had and my life would turn out
badly. I respectfully explained that I was nothing like her, but that
no matter what, she was still my mother and I forgave her. I said,
"I made my choice, Dad. I came to America to be with you knowing that you now have your own family. If I wanted to live the life
she led I would have stayed in Hungary. In spite of everything that
happened in the past, I love her and I love you and I will never
give up hope that someday you both will be at least friends again."

Dad was quiet for a while, and then he apologized for trying to
cut off my relationship with my mother. He said, "I am so sorry to
hurt you like this. I won't talk about her so negatively again. I was
just trying to look out for you." I could sense so much bitterness
in his voice. He still carried a lot of hurt from his experience with
her.

Then he spoke about his Hungarian family and those he had
lost during the war. He spoke so lovingly about his sister, Irene,
and his brother, Odon, and his young nieces and nephews who
had all been killed in concentration camps. It was obvious that he
still missed them very much.

Then he told me for the first time how he lost his right arm during his escape from the labor camp. He said, "In the camp there were rumors that Germany was losing the war. The German guards routinely got drunk at night, and they were not paying much attention to us. I was pretty fortunate because a couple of friends from our string quartet ended up in the same camp with me. Periodically, we were told to play for the officers in the evening because they knew we were musicians. Sometimes this would get us an extra ration of food or an easier workload. We talked about escaping all the time but had to find the right time to do it because we knew if we got caught we would be killed on the spot. We noticed that some of the guards just walked away from the camp and were never seen again. As things became more and more disorganized with the guards and officers, we waited for the right time to make our move.

"One night, when the guards were asleep, we were able to climb over the fence. We didn't get very far before we heard shooting all around us, so we dashed inside a nearby farmhouse to wait it out. We didn't know if they were Germans or Russians or even Americans. We could tell that they were getting close, and then there was a huge explosion. Everything went black.

"When I regained consciousness I was on a wagon bleeding very badly, and my right arm was barely attached to my shoulder. The pain was excruciating. I next remember vaguely that I was in a church that was like a makeshift hospital and there was a Russian doctor trying to stop the bleeding from my arm. He told me that my arm could not be saved. He needed to amputate it or I would bleed to death. The last thing I remember was the unbearable pain as he proceeded to saw off my arm before I passed out. I don't remember much after that. When I regained consciousness, I was in an actual hospital, where I stayed for a few weeks to recover. Eventually I was allowed to leave and return to Miskolc, where I learned that my entire family had been killed in the gas chambers in Auschwitz."

As my father was telling this very sad story he didn't sound bitter, but I could hear the pain in his voice. Hearing these stories really tore me up in my exhausted and already emotional state, but I did work up the courage to ask him the one question that had been on my mind for a very long time. "Dad, when you lost your family, lost your arm, and found the family home and business destroyed, were you tempted to end it all?"

He was quiet for a long time, and then he said, "Yes, I did think about ending my life, but only once. I was walking downtown in Miskolc trying to figure out what to do next. As I looked around I saw people with no legs; people who had lost not just one, but both arms. There were people who had lost their eyesight and hearing. I actually felt lucky that I had lost only one arm! I was truly one of the luckier ones."

He paused, and then said something that left the most profound impression on me: "When I was at my lowest point I was ready to throw in the towel. But then I remembered my strong and loving family who had such faith in me and always taught me that I could accomplish anything with hard work and perseverance. There was never a time when I didn't feel their unconditional love and support. They had never missed any of my performances, and they sat with me for hours on end watching me practice my cello. My brother and sister were always cheering me on, and my mother was always rubbing my sore fingers and bringing me fresh-squeezed lemonade. My father had such great dreams for me. The memories of their devotion and love for me gave me the hope and the strength to start over. I wanted them to be proud of me. I desperately wanted to continue their legacy. And here we are! I finally have you here with me, and I am remarried and have a little boy and another child on the way. After all these years, once again I have my family."

We stood in silence for a minute while I took it all in. Then, with conviction, he said, "You know, there is nothing more important than education! Knowledge is power! I firmly believe to this day that my knowledge of music and sharing it with my enemies saved my life."

When we got home Dad opened the closet door and motioned for me to come and look. He took out a beat-up old leather coat that I recognized immediately. It was the same one he had worn when we tried to escape from Hungary in 1956. The lining of the coat was still torn on the bottom where he had hidden the money to bring to America. He said, "Do you remember this coat?"

It was so emotional to see it again. I responded, "Yes, Daddy, I do. I remember watching you sew money into the lining while I was pretending to sleep. I wanted to help you so badly, but I thought you would be upset with me if you knew I wasn't sleeping. I was so proud of you. You could do anything with your one arm!"

I hugged my father for a long time and made a firm decision right there and then: if one day I would be lucky enough to have a family of my own, I would love my children with all my heart and soul. I would give them the values, encouragement, and the support they needed always to feel the power of my love and the love of our family. When life threw challenges at them they would survive, and even thrive, because they had been raised with strong values and the unconditional love and support of their mother and family. Even when I am no longer here for them in person, they will still feel my love for them in their hearts, and they will carry on!

We walked home after sunset and I just fell into bed, exhausted. But sleep was tough. I was going to school the next day, Monday, September 16, 1963. I had no idea what to expect. I had been in the United States for only two days.

My father and his wife, Irma on their honeymoon in San Francisco in 1961.

My new family: Dad, Irma with my precious little brothers
Robbie and Eddie in the early Spring of 1964 after 6 months
in America.

My little brothers and I before Irma got sick.

Chapter 11
HIGH SCHOOL

Dad had explained to me that high school was going to be very different from the gymnasium I had attended in Budapest. Here, nobody stopped to salute the teachers when they walked by. You didn't stand up when the teacher came into the classroom. The kids in school did not wear uniforms, and the girls dressed very provocatively (at least in my eyes!).

Many of the girls wore very tight pants or skirts that were quite short. Back home I was never even allowed to wear pants! In Hungary, only women of ill repute wore pants. The girls in America wore so much makeup that they looked a lot older than their age. I felt like an oddball, looking very plain in my uniform I brought with me from Hungary. It was a navy blue long tunic we had to wear over our dress with a removable white collar. I thought it would be appropriate to wear to school and my father and stepmother did not objec. I did not wear any makeup and I felt as if I was a kid among all these older-looking teens. Needless to say, that I never again wore my uniform to school.

My father was the head of the music program at Carpinteria High, which included the marching band, but he was not treated with the kind of reverence and respect he enjoyed in Hungary. He conducted the school's chorus and the orchestra, both of which I joined immediately. Although I didn't speak any English, I could read music and just mimic the words in chorus even though I had no idea what I was singing.

Watching him lead the marching band during football season was really hard for me at the beginning. The music was a far cry from the classical music I had grown up with. It seemed to me that nobody was really paying attention to the band during the game or even during halftime. People were busy running around getting snacks or talking to each other while the marching band was playing its heart out. Dad always lost a lot of weight during the football season because they had to practice for hours outside and most of the time the temperature was in the high nineties. To this day I still don't understand the importance of the marching band. And it was a mystery to me who came up with the name for this game—football. They didn't use their legs very often, but the guys were mostly throwing the ball and then climbed on top of one another to get the ball back from the other team. The sport seemed very violent, almost medieval to me. It was especially hard to watch when kids got injured. Dad assured me that one day everything would make sense to me. He said one day I might even *like* football.

I also couldn't believe that in America the students picked the subjects they wanted to take; back home all the subjects were predetermined and we had no electives. Had I spoken English I could have started university right away based on all the courses I had already finished in Hungary. So I chose English, American history, math, Russian (which I used to speak), chemistry, orchestra, and chorus.

The first three months were brutal. I knew nothing and I understood nothing. It felt like a very thick wall stood between me and all the people around me. In the classroom I copied everything from the blackboard every day, and at home later I sat with the dictionary all night trying to figure out what I had written!

My stepmother, Irma, was very helpful and worked with me every night. I had a binder book with lined sheets in it. Each page had twenty-six lines, which I divided into two columns and filled daily with new words from the dictionary. That was fifty-two words per day that I memorized. Irma tested me daily and helped me to make sentences with my newly learned words. My next challenge was trying to understand what people were saying to me in their fluent English. That was the hardest part. There were days when I thought that I would never understand or learn the English language.

To make things even more challenging, my second little brother, Eddie, was born on October 28, just five weeks after I came to America. Our family dynamics changed once again. We were all juggling our responsibilities while trying to adjust to one another. My father was working very hard at the high school, especially during the football season, and Irma was taking care of two babies only eleven months apart in age. I couldn't burden them with my problems of homesickness, and I had no one to talk to. I tried to help at home as much as I could, and I played with my little brothers, whom I loved very much. They were the highlights of my life during my first few months in America. I could speak Hungarian to them, and my one-year-old brother and I communicated just fine with my "baby English."

On November 22, 1963, President Kennedy was assassinated, and I was in complete shock. I thought, *What kind of country have I come to when someone can just shoot the president?* I had such a soft spot for JFK because to this day I believe that his meeting with Nikita Khrushchev in Vienna in 1961 was a crucial turning point for Eastern Europe. I also believed that this historic meeting and the improved international relations between America and the Soviet Union was a factor that helped me to get my permit to immigrate to America.

We were sent home from school as soon as the tragic news was confirmed. At first everyone was still hoping that he wasn't dead. It seemed that the whole country was glued to the television, hoping for some good news. My father liked the Kennedy family so much that he named my brothers Robert and Edward after the two younger Kennedy brothers. It was a very sad time for our country, and I wondered whether I had made the right decision to come to America. I wasn't even sure I wanted to stay here.

The turning point in learning to speak English came right after the Christmas break. My English teacher, Mr. McKown, asked us to analyze three poems by J. R. Lowell. This was a particularly difficult assignment for me because these poems were written in New England vernacular, not standard English. I spent my entire three weeks' vacation in the Santa Barbara library, memorizing and learning the meaning of every word in the assigned poems. Since we didn't celebrate Christmas at home, this was the best way for me to experience this special season. The first day back after the holiday, English was my first class. Mr. McKown walked into the classroom and immediately started asking questions about the poems we had been assigned over the break. He asked the class to explain the meaning of the word *courtin'*, which was the title of one of the poems. For the first time I actually understood the question and I knew the answer!

It was a magical moment for me. I tentatively raised my hand and he called on me (actually, he just pointed at me because he could not pronounce my name!). As I started answering the question, the entire class turned around, staring at me, and I turned red from embarrassment. My heart was beating so fast I could hardly breathe. It almost felt like being on stage. Now, it is true that when you are trying to learn a new language you will often explain the simplest things in the most complicated way because you lack the proper vocabulary. Somehow I answered his question, but he had to re-explain to the class what I had just said. Then he turned to me and said, "It is quite obvious that you are the only person in this entire class who read and studied these poems, so you get an A for the day—and I would like to see you after class."

This was the beginning of a very special friendship with Harry McKown and his wife, Betty. He became a true mentor. During my junior and senior years, I spent nearly every Monday night at their house, working to improve my English. They loved Shakespeare as much as I did, and we spent many evenings reading and discussing his plays and poetry. Per his suggestion, I started writing a journal in English to improve my writing skills. He would go through my journal, correct the grammatical errors, and explain to me what I had done wrong. I will always be grateful for this wonderful teacher and his beautiful wife for giving me so much of their time and help as I was learning the English language. I was still homesick and wasn't sure I could get used to this new life. When I shared these thoughts with Mr. McKown, he said, "Ildiko, the day you start liking America, she will like you back." I understood later that I just needed an attitude adjustment, and for me that really came with learning and understanding English.

I was a good student, and I began to associate with a group of kids who had in common that they were all university bound. There were a few exchange students in our school, mostly from South America. They had studied the English language in their country, and we all worked hard to become more fluent and learn about life in America. Some of my new American friends came from wealthy families, and often I was invited to their homes, which were like mini-palaces in my eyes and reminded me of the opulent homes I used to see in American films.

I began to learn about the structure of American society and what it meant to live in a nation based on free enterprise and free-dom of choice—a country where you could become anything you wanted to be if you set a goal for yourself and worked hard. It was such a wonderful discovery to learn that the majority of Americans were middle-class. In most households the men worked and the women stayed home raising families or maybe had part-time jobs. Most of these families were able to send their children to college, take nice summer vacations, and live comfortable lives. This was an entirely new reality compared with daily struggle of life in Hun-gary.

Dad felt that we needed additional income and urged Irma to go back to work after her maternity leave was over. I could tell that she really didn't want to go back to work and was overwhelmed from the pressures of juggling work and taking care of two tod-dlers at home. What I didn't know was that she had suffered nerv-ous breakdowns in the past and didn't function well under pressure. Her horrific experiences in the concentration camp and having been an orphan since she was four years old took its toll, and she was still struggling with mental health issues. She had taken medication for many years, but stopped when she married my father, thinking she no longer needed it.

Irma did go back to work, as head nutritionist at the Ventura County Health Department. She had a master's degree in nutrition and health and was well known and respected in her field. We had babysitters coming to the house to take care of little Robbie and Eddie, but it wasn't working out too well—the house was usually a mess and the babies dirty when we came home. One day I got a bad feeling and decided to go home from school on my lunch hour because I was worried about my little brothers. Thank goodness I did. When I walked into the house unexpectedly, the curtains were drawn and the babysitter was lying on the couch watching TV. Eddie was in the playpen and Robbie was crawling around the floor. She didn't even hear me come in. I was so upset that I threw her out and stayed home for the rest of the day to make sure my little brothers were taken care of. We had a variety of babysitters for the next few weeks, but things didn't go too well, and I could tell that Irma was as worried about my little brothers as I was.

Then Irma started acting a little strange. She would pick up the babies and carry them around the house, pacing back and forth and talking about the fact that we needed help. When I tried to help, she pushed me away. She did the same thing to Dad. We would find her walking around the house all night, and she just kept repeating the same thing over and over: "We need help, we need help." But she wouldn't let anyone near her or the babies. She would prepare their food and then forget to feed them. She would start their baths and forget to turn the water off. When I tried to talk to her, I could tell she didn't really know who I was. Dad finally realized that she was having a nervous breakdown and made arrangements for Irma to get the help she needed.

When he told her to get ready because someone was coming to help her recover, she said she was not going anywhere. She picked up both Robbie and Eddie and started carrying them around the house again. I was just afraid that she might drop one of them by accident. Dad kept his eye on her while I packed up some things I thought she might need in the hospital. I was relieved that the ambulance didn't have its siren sounding when it arrived, and that the two gentlemen who came to our door were wearing civilian clothes. They were both very kind and calm when they talked to her. Both my father and I were concerned that Irma might resist the medics and refuse to go with them. But when she heard the knock on the door, she just handed Robbie and Eddie over to me and said, "I am ready to go." She left without any altercation and was taken to the Santa Barbara Mental Hospital. We were told that they would call us as soon as they had done some tests on her.

When the door closed behind her, I watched my father literally collapse. I put the babies in the playpen and held him in my arms. He said, "I don't know how we will be able to get through this." I was crying, too, but I told him not to worry and that we would get through it together. I said, "Dad, I will take care of the babies and the house while Irma is gone. If you just tell the school what happened and bring home my daily homework, I promise that I won't fall behind. We will manage somehow. Maybe it is God's will that this is happening to us. When Irma gets better she will realize how much I love my little brothers and she will accept me and we can become a real family. When she sees that we can take care of things around here, everything will be okay. But she can't go back to work; she needs to stay home and just take care of the family."

Dad looked at me with gratitude and said, "You are so different from your mother. As I get to know you all over again, you do things that bring my father to my mind. Do you know that you and he are the only people in my family who have blue eyes? Even some of your facial expressions remind me of him. It makes me sad that you never got to meet. He was a very caring and affectionate man, and he was also a dreamer like you. Family was everything to him, too. I will never forget this day and what you are doing for us. I couldn't do this without you." I said, "Maybe that is why God wanted me to be here with you."

Slowly we got into a routine. Dad left for school in the morning while I fed and played with Robbie and Eddie. While they were napping I cleaned the house, did the laundry, and prepared dinner. When my father came home, he took care of the kids so I could spend the next several hours doing homework. After dinner it was time to bathe the boys, play a little, and then put them to bed. I will never forget those special nights. The boys shared a room, with one crib on each side of the room. After they were in bed I sat on the floor in the middle and held each of the babies' little fingers through their cribs while I sang Hungarian lullabies to them. They would hold on to my fingers so tightly until they drifted off to sleep. Sometimes they called me "Mommy," which just felt so beautiful to me. Then it was time to practice my cello for an hour or so and do some more studying before I finally fell into bed, exhausted. It was hard, but I was happy.

It felt wonderful to be needed, and I loved taking care of little Robbie and Eddie. One night, both babies fell asleep early, and Dad said, "I want to show you something." He proceeded to open a box full of letters from Aunt Olga at the orphanage. She had written to Dad regularly to keep him updated on my grades, my activities, and my character. Her letters were beautiful. She spoke very highly of me, and I was so surprised; I had always thought she hated me because she was so hard on me all the time.

Dad watched me cry as I read. He said, "I know how much you hated being in the orphanage, and I wanted you to see how much people loved you there. Someday, you'll understand that it really was the best and safest place for you to be at the time. I knew it would eventually pay off." I thanked him for sharing Aunt Olga's kind words with me.

Irma was away for about three months, and that gave my father and me the chance to grow closer and really get to know each other. I told him that Irma should not go back to work—it was too much for her with two babies at home. I also told him that he needed to be more thoughtful and take Irma on dates or bring her flowers every now and then. Dad agreed, and said he would try to be more considerate and that he definitely understood she couldn't work anymore.

I told my father that I could make some money cleaning houses on weekends and also do some babysitting because my English was getting better every day. I had learned how to clean and wax floors while I was in the orphanage, then my grandmother had taught me other housekeeping tasks. Later on I learned more about how to do things from my stepfather, Gyula, who was the most meticulous man I have ever met. When I moved in with them after they got married, I helped clean a lot as my way of thanking him for providing me a home.

My father wasn't happy with his job at Carpinteria High, and he wanted to go to a school where a high-quality music program was more appreciated. He told me that the community here did not support classical music instruction; the only thing people in town appreciated was football and the marching band. There were very few families there who valued my father's efforts to elevate music education at the high school. I was praying that some other school would discover what an asset my father could be to their music program, so that he would not have to work at this school any longer. Money was going to be tight for a while, and I promised Dad that I would start working soon so I could make some extra money and help out with my expenses.

At first Irma was allowed to come home only for an afternoon, then for a whole day, and at last she was released permanently. She was prescribed medication to combat her depression, which she needed to take for the rest of her life.

I was very excited to welcome Irma home. The whole house was sparkling clean, and I made a "Welcome Home" sign for her. I had my father get her a dozen red roses, and I had dinner ready for the family. The boys were bathed and all dressed up for her homecoming. When she walked in and the boys ran up to her, I could tell that she was pleased. When we hugged we both cried a little and she said, "Thank you for everything you've done." After that, Irma and I became very comfortable with each other.

In one really important area Irma was a huge help to me. I had been a chubby kid most of my childhood thanks to my orphanage diet, and when I came to America I was definitely overweight. I didn't think about it much until I started looking at all the catalogs we got from various department stores. I saw all the beautiful and slender models and wanted to look like them. Since Irma was very knowledgeable about nutrition and weight loss, I asked for her help. She was great about it. She took me to our family doctor for a complete physical exam and assessment.

I weighed almost 170 pounds, which was a lot for a sixteen-year-old girl who was 5'6 1/2" tall. He recommended that I lose between forty and fifty pounds, so I went on a strict calorie-controlled diet and the weight started coming off pretty fast. I also exercised and began to feel good about how I looked. By the time I started college at the University of California, Santa Barbara, I was down to 125 pounds and had started running.

I started working so I could have a little extra money for things I needed. Irma told some of the neighbors how well I cleaned our house, so I started getting calls to clean for them as well. Later, in my senior year, the mother of one of Dad's private cello students who owned a gift store needed sales help, and she offered me a job for the summer. The Santa Claus Pottery Shop was located along Highway 101 in a charming little shopping center called Santa Claus Lane. There were several other gift and souvenir shops and a couple of good restaurants there (all centered on a Christmas theme), and they attracted a lot of tourists. The little center was a landmark, with its huge Santa Claus sitting on the top of the roof, visible from the freeway. Still, traffic could be somewhat slow during the summer, and I was trying to figure out how to drum up business for our "little village." I noticed that there were several tour buses that regularly passed by on the freeway, and I thought it would be great if we could get them to stop at our center during the summer months. Then one day an unexpected opportunity came that in many ways set the course for my future.

I was invited to go to Los Angeles to meet and spend the weekend with one of Irma's cousins, Aunt Vera, and her family. Vera was a distant relative of my father as well. On the Greyhound bus from Santa Barbara to Los Angeles, I sat right behind the driver and eventually worked up the courage to ask him if he would ever stop at Santa Claus Lane for a lunch break and how I might invite tour buses to make the center a destination stop. Even with my broken English we managed to understand each other, and talked for a long time. He asked me what I could do for him in return if he would bring some of the buses to our shopping center. I blurted out that I would give him 10 percent of the total sales. I had absolutely no right to say that, but I honestly didn't think I would ever see this driver again.

Well, a couple of weeks later I was alone in the shop and out of the blue, three Greyhound buses pulled into our center. There was the driver with a big smile on his face! My little shop was overrun with customers, and I was busy selling and gift-wrapping like crazy. The whole thing seemed surreal. The shop did great, and I gave ten dollars to the driver, which was pretty good in 1964. The shop made $250, which was as much as we made during an entire week in the summer months. I was thrilled with my accomplishment, but I was also sure I would lose my job because of the money I had to give the driver. I hoped my boss would just take it out of my paycheck, though that would have been nearly the entire check!

When Lois, the owner, arrived late in the afternoon, I was still cleaning up from the noon rush. As usual, she checked the register and turned to me in utter disbelief. She asked me, "What in the world happened here?" I explained to her that I had been trying to help our summer business, and then I burst into tears telling her about the money I had given to the driver. I immediately told her that she could take it out of my pay. Lois started laughing and gave me a big hug; she told me I could have a job with her for life if I wanted it. After that she called my father and told him what I had done, and then she gave me a raise!

I also worked for a couple of weeks during Christmas and Easter break at the luggage store that Vera and her husband, Arthur, owned in Los Angeles. They knew I didn't have any money and that my father was the sole provider. They were very concerned about Irma's mental health and the well-being of my little brothers. I think they just wanted to help me out, knowing that I was cleaning houses and working in a gift shop for very little money.

They had two girls, Fran and Sandy, and we got along wonderfully. I loved working in their luggage and handbag shop and learned that I was really good at sales. Uncle Arthur taught me a lot about leather goods, and my English was improving rapidly. They were very generous to me and treated me like family. Uncle Arthur offered me a full-time job and promised me that they would pay me well. I thanked him for his kindness but opted to go college. I needed to get my education first, and of course both he and Vera understood and supported me in that decision.

I graduated with honors from Carpinteria High School; in fact, I was one of the top ten graduates out of twelve hundred students. My father was very proud, and that was the most important thing for me. I was accepted at the University of California, Santa Barbara in the summer of 1965, but I had to take a couple of algebra courses at the community college to satisfy all the prerequisite requirements for the university. This was quite an experience because I had to relearn everything in English. There were some nice guys in my class, and they were eager to help me along. By this time I was pretty slim, and I had a difficult time accepting all the attention I was getting from the opposite sex. I somehow finished both classes with a B-minus, and I was more than satisfied with that. In every class at Carpinteria High School I had received an A. I was excited and confident about starting my higher education.

I should have been ecstatic with the acceptance I found and everything I had accomplished during my two short years in America, but I was still hurting inside. I was terribly homesick and so lonely at times that I didn't think I would ever get used to the American way of life. I had so little in common with my classmates, and the whole dating scene was very different from what I had experienced in Hungary. I made wonderful progress playing cello, but I wasn't good enough to become a soloist and make a living from it, and I was afraid that Dad might be disappointed in me. I had long treasured a romantic notion that I would become a famous cellist and thus could give him back the dream he had lost during the war.

Of course, it didn't help that my mother and Gyula kept urging me to come home and promising me that things would be so different if I did. They had moved to a bigger apartment in downtown Budapest and said I would even have my own room. Sometimes I was really tempted just to get on a plane and go back home. And after Irma returned home, I thought maybe I wasn't really needed there anymore.

In spite of the fact that I had made some friends, I still had very little in common with them. I was invited to many parties, but the kids were drinking and even doing some drugs, and that scared me to death. Most of these kids came from affluent families and were on their way to college, but many of them seemed spoiled and, to my mind, not very happy. Then one of the kids in our group committed suicide. His mother found him in the garage, where he had hanged himself. His name was Patrick White. I had briefly dated his brother, Doug. I was never able to find out what made him take his own life, when his future had looked so promising.

Finally, one day I sat my father down and just poured out my heart to him. I said, "Dad, I can't do this anymore. I just don't belong here! I don't understand the culture, or the kids around me. I just don't think I can make it here. I don't think America is my home."

This was really hard for my father to hear, because we had gone through so much together and he had worked so hard to get me out of Hungary. He started stroking my head and said, "I know things have not been easy for you, but I want to ask you to do just one thing before you make a decision you may regret for the rest of your life. I want you to spend one year at the university, which is where you *will* meet the people with whom you have a lot of things in common. If, after one year, you still feel the way you are feeling right now, I will pay for your passage to go back to Hungary."

I accepted Dad's offer, and I entered the University of California, Santa Barbara, in September 1965.

Picture of me as a high school junior before my haircut.

My new look.

My 17th birthday with a group of my college bound friends.

Chapter 12
UNIVERSITY GIRL

During my freshman year in college I lived in supervised housing, and I roomed with three other girls I had never met previously. While it was a little intimidating to meet my roommates, we were all in the same boat. We all came from different backgrounds and none of us knew anything about the others, but they shared that they had all been born in America. There were two bedrooms and a double bathroom upstairs, plus a kitchen and living room downstairs. Each bedroom had two single beds and a large shared closet. I quickly started to make some good friends.

The campus was beautifully landscaped, and it was literally right by the ocean. I liked the fact that it was so close to the beach because that was one of my favorite spots to think, pray, and spend time in solitude.

My father's colleague and friend from Hungary, Dr. Erno Daniel, was the music director at the university. He was the conductor of both the University Orchestra and the Santa Barbara Symphony. Dr. Daniel's wife was Katinka, the friend who had helped my father get the job conducting the Communist Party Chorus after the war, when he was trying to rebuild his life and the Soviets had taken control of the vinegar factory. Dr. Daniel did not want to live under the Communist regime, and he had been able to get out of Hungary in 1945. He eventually made it to America, and was finally able to arrange for his wife and their young children to join him in Santa Barbara following the revolution in 1956.

I was in Dr. Daniel's music theory class, and was fortunate to be able to play cello in both orchestras. I really looked forward to my music classes and orchestra practice because it gave me a sense of familiarity as well as a sense of belonging. To see a familiar face was also comforting as I was trying to adjust to university life. It was special to me that we could speak Hungarian, and he shared with me some of his early experiences when he had first come to America.

I decided on a double major in music and linguistics. I wasn't really sure what I wanted to do with my life, and was still thinking about going back home, but I wanted to make the most of my first year at the university. I got involved in the International Relations Organization (IRO) so I could meet other foreign students with whom I had more in common, and it proved to be a good decision. I became active in as many events as possible, and I was also busy with orchestra, concerts, and my foreign-students club activities.

In the first year of school I made a very special friend, Kathy Warner, who was from Durango, Colorado. Kathy played the clarinet and we started spending a lot of time together after practice and concerts. When Kathy found out I was from Hungary, she told me her parents had helped quite a few Hungarian refugees find jobs in Colorado. Her father was a prominent trial lawyer and felt bad that America hadn't come to the aid of the Hungarian freedom fighters in 1956. He decided to help as many Hungarian immigrants as he could.

When Kathy told her parents she had a Hungarian friend, they invited me to spend Christmas vacation with them. As much as I wanted to go, I didn't have the money, and my father said we couldn't afford it. Kathy's parents immediately offered to pay my way. but my father still said no. For him, it was a matter of pride (and I also think he didn't want me to celebrate Christmas with a Christian family). Kathy's father called my father and explained to him how much it would mean to him and his family for me to spend the holiday with them. Finally my father relented and allowed me to go.

It was an unforgettable trip. We went by train from Santa Barbara to Los Angeles, and from there by another train straight to Colorado. It was a long trip, but I got to see some beautiful country, and Kathy and I had a blast on the train. We either talked or sang the whole time. Kathy's parents (and her older brother, who was also a lawyer) were waiting for us at the train station, and they greeted me with such warmth and open arms! They had a three-story home in Durango, and it was absolutely beautiful. They treated me like family, and we had some pretty interesting political discussions in the evenings. Kathy's father loved history and was a great storyteller. I was learning a lot about America and the millions of immigrants who had built this country into a beacon of freedom for the world.

They were so generous to me. They took me to some very fancy (and fun) local restaurants, where I tasted foods I'd never had before. We went sight-seeing and took the gondolas high up in the mountains, where I could see the most incredible Colorado winter landscape (I also discovered that I had a severe fear of heights— and I still do!). Kathy's family also took me to Silverton, a small ghost town next to Durango. As we were walking down the dusty streets it was as if I were in a western movie. There were still a few people living there, and they were very friendly and eager to share their stories. Most of the folks were sitting outside ready to chat with visitors or anyone who cared to talk to them. My favorite memory was meeting a very elderly man who was sitting in front of his house smoking a pipe and enjoying a sunny winter day. I had a ton of questions to ask him about the town, and he was also curious to learn about me. First of all, he knew so much about Hungary and its history that I was speechless. He had traveled all over the world and at one time had worked in Hollywood as a chef cooking for movie stars. I didn't really believe him at first, but then he invited us into his modest home and it was covered in photographs of all the famous people he had cooked for. There he was as a young man with Cary Grant, Clark Gable, Ingrid Bergman, Jack Lemon, Doris Day, Jack Benny, Bob Hope, and many more. He had moved to Silverton in his forties after he got married, and he never looked back.

My two weeks with the Warner family were such a happy time. I was so grateful for the opportunity to celebrate Christmas with them, and I hoped one day I would be able to reciprocate and do something for them.

Back at school, I got very involved in the IRO and attended
many social events. The first was a formal meeting followed by a
social mixer. I was running late so I sat down where I happened to
see one empty seat. I sat between a nerdy-looking guy on my left
and a much older-looking guy on my right. When I had a chance
to look, I noticed that the guy on my right was incredibly good-
looking and well dressed. His name was Edward Trotter. He had
come to Santa Barbara from Los Angeles to do his graduate studies.
He had recently spent two years in France and had joined the club
to meet people and practice his French. I could feel his eyes on me
when we were introducing ourselves, and I was immediately attracted to him. I left the meeting thinking that I would likely never
see him again. I was a freshman, and he was going to work on his
master's degree in French literature. Well, I was wrong!

Two days later, when I came home from school, my roommates
told me that someone named Edward Trotter had called for me
and left his phone number. I was excited to see him again, but I
was also pretty nervous because I knew I was not very good at the
whole dating thing. I had had only had one boyfriend, back in
Hungary. I didn't like the fact that in America a guy would just
kiss you on the lips after the first date. It had no meaning for me.
My relationship with Andras in Hungary had been special—when
he kissed me, it meant something! I could hear my grandmother's
voice in my head: "Kissing is very dangerous and can lead you to
do things you may regret later on." While I had some sexual fan-
tasies (mostly from movies I had seen), I remembered the life my
mother had led and didn't want any part of it just yet. Falling in
love seemed to cause nothing but pain and disappointment, and I
was not going to allow anybody to get close enough to hurt me.

I took my time calling Ed back, and he asked me for a date. We
went to dinner at a nice restaurant in Santa Barbara and had a great
time. Yes, he was very good-looking and also quite mature, so I
knew that a guy like him probably could have his way with any
girl. He might not be satisfied just to hold my hand. Ed was a perfect gentleman in the beginning, but I was right—he wanted more
than I was willing to give. He did teach me how to kiss, though,

and I was grateful for that. We did have a lot fun together, but I think he was shocked to find that I was still a virgin. He was really patient, but when I realized he had fallen in love with me I had to break it off. I was not ready to sleep with him—or anyone else—yet.

After my experience with Ed, I decided to date a bunch of people because then I could go out and have fun but still remain emotionally unattached. I wanted to keep my independence and not allow anyone into my heart. I continued to be certain that I would never get married, because I was convinced that marriages just don't work and love doesn't last a lifetime. Eventually, I got really good at dating without any emotional involvement at all. I had fun but kept them all at arm's length.

I still wasn't sure whether I wanted to spend the rest of my life in America, and I decided after my freshman year that I would go back home to Hungary and then see how I felt. I worked full-time during the summer as a research assistant for one of my professors, as a cashier at a local market, and as a waitress at a fine restaurant in Santa Barbara, saving every penny I earned for the trip. My mother and Gyula were very eager to have me back home.

One day, on my way home from campus, I ran into the president of our foreign students club, Natik Sakuti, who was a graduate student from Baghdad. Natik was waving to me, so I felt obliged to walk over and say hello. He was talking to a guy sitting on a bike, a very tall blond with a healthy suntan—the perfect California beach boy. His name was Jud Scott. I found out that they knew each other from the student housing complex where Jud lived and were friends. We chatted for a few minutes and then went our separate ways. Then I forgot all about the meeting—until a few weeks later.

My linguistics class was in the psychology building. One day, I had a free hour before my next class, and I was heading to the Student Union to get some coffee when I saw a very tall blond guy in the distance, waving at me. I wasn't sure who he was at first, but when I got closer he called me by name and reminded me of our meeting with Natik. It all came back to me. He joined me for coffee, and we had fun talking about school, his acquaintance with Natik, and his fraternity, of which I was not a fan.

Most of the fraternities had a pretty bad reputation among my friends. The guys were usually very rowdy; they drank a lot, had wild parties, and slept with a lot of different girls. When I mentioned this to Jud, he just smiled and told me I had the wrong idea about fraternities. He painted an entirely different picture. He told me about the history of Greek-based men's fraternal organizations, which dated back many years. He said it was basically a social organization, but it was also meant to promote brotherhood and the growth of young men who would take care of one another.

Jud and I started meeting occasionally at the Student Union for coffee, and I really enjoyed these encounters. He was a psychology major and also had a full-time job at Sears in Santa Barbara as an assistant credit manager. We were both putting ourselves through school, so we were two very busy people trying to make ends meet.

Then one day, Jud asked me for a date. At first I wasn't sure how I felt about it. He was definitely not my type. I mostly dated graduate students, and Jud was only a junior at the time. I thought he was too young for me. But he seemed different from the other guys his age. And he was tall and handsome and had the most wonderful voice. What impressed me most about him that he was very polite and when we were talking he listened to me so intently as if I was the most important person in the world. On our first date we went to a restaurant in Goleta. It was very noisy and a number of Jud's fraternity brothers were there, but we had a good time. What I found unsettling was that every time Jud touched me or put his arms around me, my whole body wanted to respond, and that scared me. We had maybe a couple more dates, but I stayed focused on saving my money so I could pay for the trip to Hungary.

The day before I was to leave for Europe, I got a note from my mother telling me that if I had time before I left, I should pick up some Sony radios and a few *Playboy* magazines because I could get a lot of money for them on the black market in Budapest. I ran in to Sears in Santa Barbara (where they were selling these radios), and planned to be in and out in matter of minutes. But then I heard the loudspeaker paging: "Jud Scott, telephone please!" My heart skipped a beat, and then I thought this couldn't be the same Jud Scott I knew. I ran downstairs to Electronics, grabbed four of the small Sony radios, and was in line for the cashier when I turned around and saw Jud standing there—all six feet, four inches of him. He looked very nice in a coat and tie. My heart started beating so fast I could hardly breathe. He was smiling at me, and his arms were open for an embrace. I didn't want to get too close to him because I didn't want him to know how fast my heart was beating. I told him I was in a big hurry, that I was leaving for Hungary the next morning and wasn't sure if I would come back. Jud just looked at me as if he were looking into my soul and said, "You will come back."

My heart was racing. I got out of his embrace, paid for the radios, and couldn't get out of there fast enough! I didn't understand what I was feeling, but I knew I had to get away from him. He made me feel things I had never felt before and seemed unable to control.

My special university friend, Kathy Warner during my visit to Durango, Colorado during our Christmas break.

Spectacular view of the Colorado Mountains.

Chapter 13
BACK TO HUNGARY

I left for Hungary in early November. It was still quite warm in Santa Barbara but in Europe it was already the beginning of a cold winter season. It was a long trip back to home because I needed to travel as inexpensively as possible. I flew from Los Angeles on Icelandic Airlines to Luxembourg, and from there to Koblentz, Germany. Then I took the train to Budapest. It was quite an adventure; we had an unexpected blizzard in Luxembourg, and I got stuck there overnight because the airport runway was covered with ice and the plane could not take off. I walked around town in the evening to get the feel of the city, and it was the most charming place I had ever seen. The airline put me up in a quaint little hotel along with my fellow stranded passengers. I had a great time and felt very grown up. We all ended up in the cozy bar of our hotel. The pilot of the plane joined our little group, and I have to admit he was a good-looking guy (I seemed to be always attracted to older men). He even bought me a drink and was a big flirt. I remember locking my bedroom door that night because he was coming on pretty strong. However, my mind was elsewhere.

I was so looking forward to being home and seeing my grandmother, mother, Gyula, and the whole family. And I was looking forward to seeing Andras, my first love. What would he say when he saw me now, so slim and different? Would we fall in love all over again? What would my mother and the rest of the family think of me? Would I want to stay in Hungary? There were a million questions in my head, and even though I was very tired I didn't sleep much that night.

After the long two-and-a-half-day journey, I finally arrived at the Nyugati Train Station in Budapest on a very rainy winter day. I was exhausted but full of anticipation. I was excited to walk all over the city again and go to my favorite spots. My mother and

Gyula were waiting for me anxiously, and we had a very tearful reunion. When we got into the cab to go home, all of a sudden everything seemed so small to me. The avenues and boulevards that had been so big in my memory seemed miniature compared to everything I had experienced in America, though I did appreciate more than ever the gorgeous architecture in Budapest. It was like being in Disneyland, walking through the old sections of Buda.

I was looking forward to seeing my parents' new apartment, and it was indeed very beautiful, right in the center of Pest. And I had my own room! It was actually Gyula's study, but they converted it into my room for my visit.

The two people I wanted to see right away were my grandmother and Andras. Mom told me that Grandmother's heart was not very good, and they didn't want to tell her in advance that I was coming home because they were afraid the excitement of anticipating my arrival might be too much for her.

We talked late into the night, drinking my mother's wonderful espresso coffee, until I just could not keep my eyes open any longer. When I woke up early the next morning, I heard my precious grandmother's familiar voice: "Where is she? I know she is here! I saw her in my dream!" I jumped out of bed and ran out to hug my tiny grandmother. She was even smaller than before. We cried and laughed for the longest time. She kept telling me that I was too thin, but very pretty. I told her I would be home for a while, so we would see each other a lot. It was so good to be with her, to hug her and share stories about America, my father, and my two little brothers.

Since the last time I had seen her, my grandfather had passed away, and she was pretty lost without him. She had her own little apartment now, but she seemed very restless. She had spent her entire life helping others, and now she was mostly by herself. She was truly a special servant of the Lord.

This time with my grandmother was so precious to me. I will remain eternally grateful to her for loving me unconditionally. She never failed to tell me that I was special and that Jesus loved me and had special plans for my life. She was always so convincing that I really believed her!

Then Andras called to welcome me home. We met the next day at the Astoria Hotel, and I still remember what I wore: a fitted forest green and black color-block jersey dress with black patent leather high heels. My hair was up in a French twist, and I thought I looked pretty good. When I walked into the lobby of the hotel, Andras was sitting in a large armchair facing the entrance. He looked very handsome and grown-up in his postman's blue glen plaid three-piece suit. His blond hair was still as curly and unruly as before. He jumped up and ran toward me, and then he just stopped. He stared at me for a minute, then took my hands and kissed both of them before we hugged and exchanged kisses. He kept looking at me and repeating, "You are so beautiful," over and over again. The whole meeting seemed like a scene out of a movie, but I knew instinctively that although we both still liked each other, the romance was gone. We went to a local Hungarian restaurant and talked late into the night. He was in film school, studying to become a film and theatrical director. I saw him one more time afterward, and that was that.

My mother and Gyula had many things planned for my visit. We traveled all over Hungary and visited many of my favorite spots. And everywhere we went they always had a guy there for me to meet. I think Mom thought that if I fell in love with someone while I was home, I would be sure to stay. I had a great time and had some wonderful dates, but no one ever came close to touching my heart.

There was one young man named Feri who still stands out in my memory. We were introduced by mom and Gyula. He was the head waiter in one of the five-star restaurants in Budapest and was also taking some engineering courses at the university. He was nice enough and treated me like a princess, but he also came on to me really strong. He kept telling me that because he didn't know how long I was going to be home, he was doing everything possible to make me fall in love with him. The strange thing was that he reminded me so much of Jud Scott. He was blond, tall and slim, but not as well-built as Jud. He was very much a take-charge kind of a guy and would have done anything for me. Unfortunately, I didn't feel anything for him even when I tried to respond to his romantic advances. Finally, I just could not see him anymore. Mom was disappointed.

One highlight of the trip was when I hosted a big dinner at Matyas Tavern, a family favorite. I wanted to see everybody all at once, and I was also curious to see everyone's reaction when they saw me looking so different from that sixteen-year-old girl who had left Hungary three and a half years earlier.

The evening was everything I had hoped for. All my aunts and uncles were there with their significant others. I was especially looking forward to seeing my cousin Agi, who was always the family favorite. Her parents were the only couple among my mother's siblings who had stayed married. She was a pretty girl and had a far more privileged upbringing than I did. But she started dating very young and got into all kinds of trouble. I was glad I was still a virgin even though many people had probably thought I would end up on the street because of the way I grew up. Well, thank God I was able to prove them wrong!

It was strange to sit there with everyone and remember what my life had been like three and a half years before. America had given me the opportunity to work three jobs at the same time, pay for school and support myself, and go to university. I had bought my tickets for the trip and had saved a thousand dollars for spending money while I was home. And in 1967 and 1968 the dollar was king all over Europe, so my money went a long way (I also sold the radios and *Playboy* magazines that Mom had told me to bring).

The three months in Hungary went fast, and then it was decision time. I needed to get back to America if I didn't want to miss the beginning of the new semester. Mom was begging me to stay. She kept telling me that the past haunted her every day and that she wanted to be the mother I deserved. She really believed we could still make up for all the time we lost and forget the past. I knew it was too late for that, but I could never say so to her.

I decided I would go back to finish school in America, but I said to Mom, "It is a long train ride back from Budapest to the border.

When it's time to cross the border, I will make my decision. If it's too hard to leave, I will get off the train, turn around, and come back. If not, I will send you a telegram to let you know that I arrived in America safely."

I went to visit Grandmother one more time, but I didn't tell her I was leaving again. It would have been too hard on her. Knowing how intuitive she was, I figured she probably knew it already anyway. When we hugged good-bye, she told me to be good and that I had a guardian angel watching over me all the time. I stood there watching her get on the bus, and then she was gone. This was a hard moment. I loved her so much, and I knew it was probably the last time I would ever see her.

Grandma passed away from a heart attack less than a year later, in 1968. I received a telegram from my mother giving me the sad news about my beloved grandmother's passing. She has remained one of the most important and powerful influences in my life beside my father.

I was eager to get on the train and be alone with my thoughts. Mom and Gyula were both crying. Finally, I just broke away, grabbed my suitcase, and got on the train. I cried on and off during the entire ride. My heart was aching so much I could barely breathe. I loved my country, and the countryside was breathtakingly beautiful! Why did I have to make such hard choices between family and country? Where did I really belong? What was God's plan for me? I was in deep thought and prayer when we got to the border.

The appearance of the border patrol guard in his uniform jolted me out of my prayers. He asked for my documents and then asked me if I'd had a good time in Hungary. I said, "I had a wonderful time." Then he asked, "Have you visited other parts of the country besides Budapest?" For some reason I lied to him and said, "No I didn't. I pretty much stayed around Budapest." He gave me a long look, and said, "Really?" Then he took out a small notebook from one of his pockets and read aloud all the places in the country I had visited, in chronological order.

For a moment I thought I was busted and would end up in jail for lying. What I said next surprised even me because it just came out of my mouth unexpectedly: "Well, I figured I didn't have to keep track because you would know where I had been even better than I." He just looked at me with a smug smile on his face and said, "Okay, young lady, have a good trip."

I couldn't get through the border fast enough. Just the thought that someone had been watching me during those three months at home felt very creepy, and all I wanted was to get back to America as fast as possible! God had made the decision for me. When I finally landed at Los Angeles International Airport, I wanted to kiss the ground!

This time everything looked familiar to me. I was no longer a complete stranger and had a new sense of belonging that I had never felt before. For the first time I understood that America was truly the land of the free, and I felt a genuine love and appreciation for this country. It was time to change my attitude, stop looking back, and open my mind and heart to all the opportunities America had to offer. This was a major turning point in my life.

My father was at the airport to pick me up, and I could tell he was relieved to see me. I knew he was glad that I had decided to make America my permanent home. We had a long talk, just sharing some of our experiences about adjusting to life in America. It had also been very hard for him to adjust, especially at the beginning when he didn't know anybody. Because he had only one arm, he was considered handicapped, so finding a job teaching music had taken some time. But he knew he could not live in Hungary under the oppression of the Communist Party, and he was deeply grateful for the opportunity to build a new life in America.

After I went to college, my father with his family moved up the California coast a little way to San Luis Obispo in 1966 and began his job as music director for San Luis Obispo High School, where he enjoyed great success and was loved by the faculty and parents alike. He was very happy there, and loved that music education became a primary focus of the district. He was also involved in community efforts and did some prison outreach. He brought music appreciation to the prison at Soledad, and his visits were well received by the prisoners. They all loved the one-armed gentleman with the heavy accent who brought the joy of music into their lives. Dad always believed that music lifted you up and made you a better person, and he really enjoyed his prison ministry.

By the time Dad moved to San Luis Obispo in 1966, life had changed for the worse for his old friend Fred Balazs. When his wife left him and abandoned their children, Fred did his best to provide for them, but once they were grown he was alone. Dad invited him to move to San Luis Obispo and gave his old friend a place to live free of charge in one of the apartments Dad owned. Soon after, my father opened the San Luis Obispo Conservatory of Music, and Fred became one of the head music instructors.

Then they were together every day. My father would go for his daily morning swim at 6:00, and then he and Fred would have their favorite Hungarian breakfast together which consisted of fresh fruits, and rye toast with dry salami on special occasions. They made each other laugh and sometimes could even joke about the misery they had experienced at the labor camp. They shared the joy of teaching young children how to play the cello, bass, violin, flute, clarinet, and so on. They created the most wonderful children's orchestra the community had ever had. Their annual children's concert became a very popular annual event attended by hundreds of people every year.

It was an amazing friendship that survived the horrors of the Holocaust. Fred then helped my father to get his very first job in Tucson; later my father was there for Fred and helped him out in the autumn of his life in San Luis Obispo, when he had nowhere to turn. After my father's passing, Fred moved back to Tucson, where he continued to compose music and was a guest conductor for the Tucson Symphony into his late eighties.

Chapter 14
JUD

I was happy to resume my college life. By this time I lived in an apartment with three girls, and when I got back the first thing they told me was that there was a really cute guy named Jud from the Phi Kappa Psi fraternity who had been calling for me and wondering when I would be back. They also said he drove a very cool convertible car. I told them I don't usually call guys, but they kept urging me on; so finally I agreed, just to get them off my back. Besides, I figured there were some sixty or more guys living in the fraternity house, so it wasn't likely I would even talk to Jud.

I dialed the number to the house, and when I heard someone pick up I said, "May I speak with Jud, please?" There was a moment of silence and then I heard a beautiful, deep voice say, "Ildiko, is that you? Where are you?" I barely had a chance to respond before Jud said, "I'll be right over."

Out of all those guys, how could he possibly be the one to answer the phone? Was this just a coincidence, or was it God's intervention? The minute I saw Jud, my heart was racing, and those unsettling emotions I had felt for him before came back stronger than ever. I promised myself I would just see what happened, and would not allow this guy take control of my heart. I was going to date a bunch of other guys, just to keep clear of any serious involvement.

We did go on several dates, and Jud was always a gentleman (though the rest of his fraternity brothers were not). In spite of the fact that he was only eighteen months older than me, he seemed very mature and extremely smart. I loved listening to his deep, commanding voice. His six foot four inches frame towered over me, and I always felt safe being with him. I found Jud very attractive even though he was so different from all the other young men I dated—and that scared me even more. We were able to talk about everything, our lives, our goals, our future aspirations. The way he looked at me, and some of the things he said were so romantic and sweet that I actually felt beautiful. Every time I said good bye to Jud I told myself that I needed to stay away from him.

I still remember the evening when I realized I was in trouble. He took me on a special date before we went to his fraternity Christmas party in an exclusive mansion in Montecito. The restaurant was called Somerset. It was a very expensive five-star restaurant, especially for a guy who was putting himself through college.

I could tell that Jud wanted it to be a perfect evening, but little things kept happening that seemed humorous to me, though I am sure Jud didn't think so. When he came around the car to open my door, he tripped; I pretended not to see it. We had reservations at the restaurant, but the place was really busy, so we got probably the worst table for two, between the kitchen and the bar. It was obvious that we were two college kids trying to act very grown-up in this five-star restaurant which more than likely was way over our budget. The waiters were running by us as if we didn't exist. I could tell Jud was uncomfortable because he wanted everything to go well. I enjoyed every minute just observing him trying to be such a gentleman. He tried so hard to have a meaningful conversation, while I was just staring at him. I wanted to kiss him a thousand times so he would stop trying so hard to impress me. It reminded me of the television show *To Tell the Truth:* I wanted to say to Jud, "Will the real Mr. Scott please stand up?"

During dinner Jud told me that he had joined the navy, and right after graduation he was leaving for Officer Candidate School (OCS). I knew that America was deeply involved in the war in Vietnam, but I didn't know much about the military here. I was aware that they were drafting young men to go to war at the university, so Jud had decided to sign up before he was drafted. At first I was a little sad, but in truth I was also relieved, because the feelings I felt around him were so strong that they scared me. I wanted to be free again and be in control of my heart at all times.

After dinner we went to the fraternity party at the fancy mansion, and we drank and danced a lot. I loved dancing, but I think

Jud mostly enjoyed the slow dances, when he held me close and we kissed. Here were those feelings again. Every time he kissed me, my head would spin. I was so afraid to lose control of my feelings that I kept trying to reassure myself by thinking he was leaving soon, and I would break it off and go on with my life.

When the time came for Jud to leave for OCS, he wanted to come over to say good-bye. I decided that I simply could not see him again and told my roommates that when he came over, they had to tell him I wasn't home. I will never forget hiding in my bedroom closet and hearing the disappointment in his voice when they told him I wasn't there. It took all the willpower I could muster not to run out of the closet and into his arms. He brought back a book he had borrowed (*Nicholas and Alexandra*, a historical fiction about Russia at the turn of the twentieth century) and told the girls that he would be in touch. And then he was gone. I did feel some guilt for a moment, but I reminded myself of my promise to myself that no man would ever control my heart. After I was sure he was gone, I went for a long run. That always seemed to be the best thing to do when my feelings got too intense. Running every day was my salvation and solitude. I ran until I couldn't run anymore, and then I was back to my old independent self again.

I went back to my busy life. I was doing well in college, and I worked part-time at the same three jobs I'd had before leaving for Hungary: cashier at our off-campus village market, occasional research work for my linguistics professor, and waitressing at El Paseo restaurant in Santa Barbara. I began dating a lot of guys—nothing serious, except for one guy who became pretty significant in my life for a short time. His name was Hormuz Motamedi. We had briefly met at a social event for my foreign students club. He was getting his doctorate in electrical engineering and was a gorgeous man. He was exactly the type of man I was always attracted to: tall, dark, and dangerously handsome.

I never thought a guy like that would ever look at me, but he did, and I fell for him big-time. But it wasn't anything even close to the feelings I'd had for Jud. I think I was excited to find out that the guy everyone would have loved to date picked me and would not look at anyone else. Hormuz was in the United States from Iran and had two brothers here as well who had both married an American girls. His mother had left his father in Tehran because he was very domineering and she wanted to make something of herself independently of him. They left their homeland for many other reasons.. Hormuz wanted to get his Ph.D. in electrical engineering in an America and wanted to be close to his two older brothers. They were also very aware that the Shah had lots of enemies in Iran and there was a lot of unrest during his leadership. The Shah was a great friend to the United States and that made him very unpopular among the more traditional leaders in Iran. While Hormuz was happy to be in America, he was very much a traditional Middle Eastern man (though his admiration for his mother's independence was one the things that attracted me to him).

We dated for a whole year, and I was really debating how far to go with the relationship. He had fallen in love with me, and I was very attracted to him physically. I often wondered what the whole sex thing was all about. Was it as wonderful as people said it was? Movies always glamorized sex. I was curious to find out if it really was all that great. It was important to me to remain morally strong; however, having made up my mind that I would probably never marry, I thought I might as well find out what I was missing. I was twenty-one years old, and I don't think anyone believed I was still a virgin.

One night Hormuz took me to a very romantic dinner at the Santa Barbara Inn. He kept writing "Dusat Daram" on his napkin over and over, which means "I love you" in Persian. I decided that I was ready and tonight would be the night to take the next step. At least I knew he would be considerate, and maybe even a little shy. One thing was certain—I had no idea what I was doing. When he took me to my apartment and kissed me good-night, I told him to come in because I knew that my roommates were away. He cautioned, "No, I can't because it is just too hard for me to be with you and not have you." I said, "Tonight is the night, if you still want me." For some reason I was very calm, but I could tell that Hormuz was so nervous I almost felt sorry for him. He stayed with me that night, and I felt very grown-up the next day.

I tried to analyze my feelings. I thought that sex was okay but not anything to go completely crazy over. I think what amazed me more than anything was that Hormuz seemed more in love with me than before. After that, things began to change. He became very possessive and jealous. At first I was flattered by all the attention, but later on I became scared and needed to get away from him.

In the meantime, Jud was writing me letters from OCS. The romantic tone scared me off, and I wrote him a "Dear Jud" letter to simplify my life. When I got intimate with Hormuz, that was all I could handle. And then one day everything changed.

I was working the late shift at the Village Market. Just before closing, the market usually got very busy because people would come in for their midnight snacks. This was 1968, with the hippie movement in full bloom and the drug culture exploding. It was all very confusing for me. These young people did not love America, and they did not work hard to get a good education. What were they trying to accomplish by smoking dope and partying hard or sitting around talking about different ideologies, none of which made any sense to me whatsoever? All I wanted to do was get a good education, get my degree, and make my father proud of me. There were constant demonstrations against the Vietnam war, and they were burning the American flag. This just made me cry. I often thought of Jud and prayed he would be safe and not be aware of all the crazy things going on at our school and all over our country.

Marijuana and LSD were the drugs of choice at the time, and that apparently made people very hungry, especially late at night. Kids would come and buy everything in sight, especially junk food like chips and cookies and, for some reason, chocolate milk. This particular night, as usual, I was swamped at midnight. All of a sudden, there were three or four men from Jud's fraternity at the entrance of the market, looking in. When I looked up I could not believe my eyes. Jud was standing there, smiling at me! I think my heart just stopped for a minute, and I thought I was dreaming.

He looked very handsome, and I didn't know what to do. We just stared at each other, and I forgot about everything and everyone around me! All I know is that this man seemed to take control of my heart the minute he showed up in my life. When I regained my composure, I could tell that the people in line knew there was something special going on. They probably expected me to jump over the counter into Jud's arms! Finally, Jud asked if he could see me after work. I wanted to say yes so badly, but I was being picked up so I told him to come over for breakfast the next morning. It was very difficult to finish my shift and spend the night with Hormuz.

I left Hormuz's place at 6:00 a.m. and ran to the market to get some food, then raced home to my apartment to prepare breakfast. I was so nervous that my hands were trembling when Jud arrived. I decided to tell him that I was dating somebody and all was well. But I could hear a voice in my head telling me, "You are in love with this guy. What are you doing? This is the real thing! What are you afraid of?"

As we were sitting across from each other at the kitchen table, I remember Jud never stopped smiling at me while I was talking. The couple of hours we spent together catching up on our lives went by too fast, and then Jud had to leave. He was now a junior officer in the navy and had just finished submarine school in Connecticut before driving across country. He had stopped in Santa Barbara to visit his old fraternity brothers. He needed to drive home to drop off his car and say good-bye to his parents near San Francisco, and then he would be on his way to Japan to join his new submarine on a lengthy deployment.

I will never forget his words to me when we were at the door saying our good-byes: "Ildiko, I have known you on and off for almost three years. I didn't really know what you needed, but I do now, and I am ready to love you." Then he took me in his arms and started kissing me. I reciprocated willingly, and was completely lost in his embrace. I remember stammering something like that I was glad I had postponed our visit the night before because I would have been in big trouble.

Everything felt so different with Jud. When we kissed I felt as if my heart just opened up. I was so happy with him. When he held me in his arms and his skin touched mine, I felt safe and whole. It seemed to me as if he didn't hear anything I said about having a boyfriend and that my life was going well. It really didn't matter now, because my reaction to Jud was so natural and real that there were no more words needed.

I could no longer deny that I was hopelessly in love with Jud Scott and that somehow I had to end things with Hormuz. My heart was taken, and I wanted to stay true to Jud. I got some very romantic letters from him, but then nothing for a while because he was at sea.

One day I received a huge envelope full of letters. Jud had written to me almost every day while at sea, although he couldn't mail them until he returned to port. His letters made my heart stop. I remember I would run to the mirror and look at myself and then look at these letters, wondering what it was that he saw in me. What if he really got to know me and didn't love me anymore? I had seen how relationships could implode and how people in love often ended up hurt, especially after they married. Then I received a little package from Jud, and inside was a small silver box. When I opened the box there was a beautiful ring, with two round black corals and three white pearls surrounding them. He enclosed a card that said, "Black coral is very rare and found only in deep water; they are you and I. The three white pearls are faith, love, and compassion. The gold band represents our golden future. May these ideals lead us in our lives. Love, Jud." Then I received a dozen yellow roses from him!

I was overwhelmed with emotion and knew I had found my fairy-tale prince. During all this time I tried to see Hormuz as little as possible, but he became more and more demanding of my time. I was scared because I didn't want to hurt his pride, but I also had no idea how to break up with him.

Then, in December, I received an unexpected Christmas card from Jud. Inside the envelope was a plane ticket to Hawaii with a card attached: "Would you like to be my Christmas present? Love, Jud." I was standing there in shock because I had promised I would go to Los Angeles with Hormuz for a New Year's party and spend time with his friends and his mom. I didn't find out until much later that he had planned to propose to me on New Year's Eve.

What was I going to do? Thank God my roommate Susan was home at the time, and I shared my dilemma with her. She said, "Forget Los Angeles! You must go to Hawaii and make a decision once and for all what is really in your heart!" Susan was a good Christian girl, and she wasn't a fan of me dating a Muslim, even though he wasn't religiously observant (my father and Irma weren't happy either with the knowledge that I was dating a Muslim man).

Then Jud called and asked me if I had gotten his card and the plane ticket and wanted to know if I could come to Hawaii. My intention had been to tell him that I would really love to see him, but I had already made other plans. But hearing his voice over the phone, I knew my heart belonged to him. Finally, after we talked for a while about our feelings, I told him I would try to be there the next day. Interestingly, neither Jud nor I really remembers much of our conversation, and we don't know what he said that changed my mind so quickly. After I hung up the phone I just sat there and had absolutely no idea how I would be able to get out of town without letting Hormuz know. Luckily, my wonderful roommate was there to save me; she promised to cover for me.

I must have looked very helpless, because Susan looked at me and took charge. "I have been to Hawaii many times," she said. "You can borrow some of my clothes, since we wear the same size. We are leaving campus right now and will stay at my parents' house tonight. We will take you to the airport tomorrow morning." I just kept saying, "Thank you," over and over. I was in such a daze wondering how Hormuz would feel about me just disappearing without notice. But I also knew that I had to see Jud, and this time I was not going to disappoint him.

God sometimes puts people in our lives at just the right time, and we have to simply follow his plan. Susan was such an angel. She practically packed my suitcase for me, because I was such a basket case! I called my parents and told them about my travel plans, and they were pleased that I was not spending the holiday with Hormuz. Dad was a little concerned about my "sleeping arrangements" in Hawaii, but I assured him that Jud was a perfect gentleman and there was nothing to worry about.

Until my plane took off from the Santa Barbara airport, I was afraid that somehow Hormuz would find me and keep me from leaving. I didn't sleep at all that night, and instead spent a lot of time praying and asking God to show me some kind of sign that I was making the right decision. In my heart I knew I was!

The flight seemed to take only minutes. I was deep in thought and prayer the entire time. Part of me was terrified that I was making a big mistake—after all, I didn't really know Jud. At the same time, I recalled his loving words, his beautiful love letters, and the way it felt when we kissed. I remembered the way he looked at me and how he always treated me as if I were the most important person in the world.

Roses from my very romantic future husband.

The handsome young Jud I fell in love with.

One of my favorite photos of Jud during his Submarine WestPac
Tour; in Hong Kong at the Victoria Peak Cafe.

Chapter 15
TRUE LOVE

I landed at the Honolulu airport, and Jud was waiting for me with open arms and the biggest smile on his face. He draped a lovely Hawaiian lei around my neck (which is how people welcome visitors there), and then we hugged and kissed it seemed like for several minutes. I wanted to stay in his arms forever; it felt so right.

There was no question in my heart that I was in love with Jud, and just from the way he looked at me it was obvious that he was in love with me. I still remember that we kissed at every red light, hoping it would never turn green. I kept telling myself, "You can't lose your head! You are still in a relationship that has to end first! Stay true to yourself and if you really love this man, do the right thing!" But being in Hawaii, the most beautiful place on Earth, just made me fall even harder for Jud. And he had such a way with words. He always said the most romantic things, things that made my head spin. I thought he must have been reading romance novels because it seemed as if his words were out of a book. Later on I learned that this was just how he really was. He could express his feelings to me in a way that always made me feel loved.

We spent time with Jud's sister, Sandee, and her fiancé, Craig, who were also there visiting. We liked each other right away and had a lot of fun together. We spent New Year's Eve in Honolulu in a cabin on the beach, and it was wonderful. We slept on the beach under the beautiful Hawaiian sky and woke up late with the sun shining right above us. I remember Jud saying sweet things like, "Would you like to live here someday?" Of course, I said yes, thinking that though it would never happen, it was still fun to think about.

As Jud was now a lieutenant, we were allowed to stay at some of the navy facilities, which made the trip a lot more affordable and also very memorable. After we toured the highlights of Hon-olulu, we flew over to the Big Island with Sandee and Craig and stayed in the most romantic cottages in Kilauea Military Camp, which is located within the Volcanoes National Park. It was haunt-ingly beautiful there. A constant flow of steam wafted up through some cracks on the ground, making everything look mysterious, and of course we were surrounded by the tropical forest. It seemed to me that the soil in Hawaii was so fertile that anything could grow there. The vegetation was lush and gorgeous. I have never seen so many shades of green, and flowers grew everywhere.

Jud was an incredible tour guide. He knew everything about the craters as well as the history of the Hawaiian Islands. We toured and hiked all over the Big Island, and I was ready to leave everything behind and stay there forever. The nights were the hardest because I knew that no matter how much I wanted to give myself to this man, I just could not do it yet. I think I was afraid that if I gave in I could become like my mother, who was able to handle several different relationships simultaneously. That just wasn't me!

One night, we were walking back to our cabin after dinner and a tropical storm came out of nowhere. We almost could not see where we were going. Jud just grabbed my arm and gently pulled me inside the camp's old fire station and said, "Let's wait out the storm here. It usually lasts only a few minutes." It was a very warm and humid night, and the rain actually felt wonderful on my skin. Once inside the fire station, Jud was holding me in his arms as we were watching the rain as we stood next to one of the fire trucks. The next thing I knew, Jud said, "I love you, Ildiko. Will you marry me?" I was speechless at first, but then I said yes, even though I didn't really know what I was committing myself to. I remember thinking, *I love this guy so much that even if we don't work out at least I'll know what being in love feels like.*

I told Jud everything about my relationship with Hormuz and promised I would end it as soon as I got back. In my heart I was scared about what might have happened while I was away. I think Jud knew I was not looking forward to returning to campus. Nevertheless, he encouraged me to be strong, and his love gave me strength. If he was concerned at all about me going back and facing my "boyfriend," he didn't show it; I think he now realized that my heart belonged to him. Saying good-bye at the airport was very emotional because neither of us wanted to part. It was hard to leave Jud and this beautiful island, especially knowing what I had to face when I got back to school.

The plane ride back to the mainland was a blur. I was oblivious to everything around me. I was trying to assess everything that had happened between Jud and me. While there was no question whether I was in love with him, the word *marriage* weighed heavily on my heart. I simply could not shake the memories of all I had seen as a child, and I didn't want history to repeat itself. Perhaps the hardest part for me was to accept being loved. And no one made me feel more loved than Jud.

Susan picked me up at the airport and told me everything that had happened while I was gone. Apparently, Hormuz came to get me, and when no one was home he broke into the apartment through the window. When Susan came home and told him that I'd had to go out of town unexpectedly, he went crazy. When he asked where I went, Susan said she had no idea because I hadn't shared any details with her. A few days later, he apparently attempted to commit suicide. He was still in the campus infirmary in recovery when I got home. I went to see him right away, and told him that I would be around to help him get better but could no longer be his girlfriend.

We talked about our cultural and religious backgrounds, and I wanted him to understand the reasons why our relationship would never work. I also told him that I could never forget that he was the first man I had been intimate with and that I would have that memory forever. I thanked him for being so good to me and wished him well. I did visit him a few more times while he was recovering, but there was no intimacy between us ever again.

I was now in my senior year, but I had to stay an extra semester to graduate because of my long trip to Hungary. It was a very busy time; I was still working three jobs while taking a full load of classes. I had shifted from my previous the waitressing job to working as a cocktail waitress at a restaurant in Montecito. (Oddly enough, it was the very restaurant where Jud and I had our first formal date.) I think the perspective I had coming from such a different cultural background inspired me to work even harder in America. I was grateful that I was independent and that I could take care of myself without help from my parents.

It was good to be so busy because it made the time pass quickly. Jud was coming home on a two-week leave in early spring, and I was counting the days until I could see him again. I was so excited about his visit because I was now free to let my guard down and show him how I really felt. The idea of opening my heart to him was still very frightening to me, but then I would remember how God had kept bringing us together, and I knew that He had a special plan for us.

I wanted to have a welcome home party for Jud that included all his fraternity brothers. I knew he would want to stop by the house and reconnect with his friends. In the past, I had given him such a hard time about fraternities that I thought having a special surprise party would make up for some of my unkind remarks. Susan helped me plan the party and prepare all the food. Jud's fraternity brothers were really looking forward to seeing him. They were ready to have some fun and, as usual, they provided the alcohol.

I was nervous and excited when I picked up Jud at the Santa Barbara airport. I remember I had to ask him to drive back to campus because my legs were shaking so badly that I could not keep my feet on the gas pedal! After we got back to my apartment everything happened so naturally, as if we had belonged to each other for a long time. As soon as the door was closed behind us, we started kissing and Jud carried me into my bedroom where we made love for the first time. While I was a little self-conscious, everything felt so right. I remember looking into his eyes, and all I saw there was tenderness and love!

If it had been up to Jud we would have stayed in the apartment for the rest of the night, but I had to get him out of there before all his friends started arriving. I told him I wanted to show him all the special places on the beach where I used to sit and read his beautiful letters. He was a good sport about it and let me take him to all my favorite spots. It was so romantic lying next to him on the beach, talking, kissing, and sharing all the things that had happened to us since our time in Hawaii.

After a while we walked back to my apartment, where I knew his fraternity brothers would be waiting. Jud was blown away when I opened the door and all his friends yelled, "Surprise!" Everybody had a great time, and I was really happy because I could tell Jud was very pleased that I would do this for him. It was late by the time everyone left, and we went to bed tired but very happy. I fell asleep in Jud's arms, feeling so secure and complete. I had never felt like this before. The next day we were on our way to San Luis Obispo to meet my family. He wanted to ask my father formally for my hand in marriage.

My father and Jud hit it off from the moment they met. When Jud asked for his blessing, Dad happily gave his approval. My little brothers were seven and eight at the time, and they were crazy about Jud from the start. In the morning they were up early waiting for him to wake up so they could play roughhouse. I told them Jud was very tired and they needed to give him a little more time to sleep. The bedrooms were all upstairs, so they sat patiently on the staircase by his room until I gave them the okay. Then they ran into his room and jumped on the top of the bed with great enthusiasm. Jud was so wonderful about it, and he bonded with the boys very quickly.

I slept on a sofa bed downstairs so Jud could have some privacy and sleep in my old room. When everyone was in bed already, my father came downstairs and sat on the edge of my bed. He told me that he was impressed with Jud and said he felt I had made a very good choice. And then he said something else that meant more to me than anything in the world: "You know, I was very concerned that you might be making some bad choices because I know what you were exposed to back home. Having met Jud, and seeing all that you have accomplished in such a short time, I am so proud to say that you are my daughter." He also told me that I shouldn't tell Jud everything about my early childhood, especially my crazy life with my mom, her incarceration, the orphanage years, and so on. When I asked my father why I should keep any secrets from the man I planned to spend the rest of my life with, he replied, "He thinks you are perfect, and I don't want him to think of you differently when he finds out about how you grew up." I didn't say anything to Dad, but I felt deeply hurt inside and decided right there and then that I would tell Jud everything there was to know about me. If that was going to change his feelings for me, so be it. I had never thought I would marry anyway, so I was ready to face the consequences of my actions.

After meeting my family, we drove north to Sunnyvale to meet Jud's parents. He shared with me some things about his mother, Jean, who sounded just wonderful, and his father, with whom he didn't have much of a relationship at all. I met his younger sister, Carol, and they were all very kind to me. Jean and I connected immediately; I loved her right away. I could tell that as soon as she saw her son so happy, I could do no wrong in her eyes. We stayed with them for only one night and then went to a hotel in Millbrae for the remaining week before Jud had to rejoin his submarine. We toured all over San Francisco and spent some time with Sandee and Craig again. They were engaged to be married on November 28, 1970, and our wedding date was set for the following spring.

The time with Jud was amazing. We talked and talked about everything. I left nothing out, waiting to see if there were changes in the way he felt about me, but I saw only love in his eyes. He shared everything with me also. In a way we had a lot in common. He grew up in a home with an intact family but one without closeness and affection. His father, Jerry, was an only child who followed in his father's footsteps and joined the Navy and worked his way up to commander. His father was a mechanic on one of the destroyers and was gone during most of Jerry's formative years. He died very early, at age fifty-three. His mom, Buzzy, was a nice lady, but she was not very maternal. Like my mother, she loved to party. As a result, Jerry grew up with little affection and attention from his parents. He fell in love with my mother-in-law, Jean, who was also an only child. They were happily married until she got pregnant with Jud, their first child.

Jean loved being a mom and threw herself into taking care of her little boy. She apparently ignored Jerry, unfortunately, and that caused a lot of resentment toward Jud. They never really developed a healthy father-and-son relationship. I think the hardest thing for Jud was that he never received any approval or praise from his parents for the things he accomplished, in school or anywhere else. His sisters, Sandy and Carol, fared better with Jerry because they were not competition for him in the same way. Being a military family, they moved around a lot, so Jud never really had a chance to make any close friends—at least until they moved to Sunnyvale in northern California, where he met a wonderful young man in high school named Dick MacDonald. They became close friends, and remain so to this day. Dick also joined the navy; he married a very special lady, Cheri, and they have been with us during some of the most important moments in our lives. Dick was one of five brothers, and Jud spent a lot of time at the MacDonald home during his high school years. It was a lot happier place to be than his own home, and Dick's family was very accepting of Jud. Jud could be very social but basically he was a loner and very self-sufficient.

The more Jud and I talked, the more I loved this man; but the whole marriage thing was still very scary to me. I still feared that once we were married, things would change drastically and our love and passion for each other would vanish. When I tried to verbalize these things to Jud, he just laughed and said, "I will love you just the way you are and will make love to you even when I am an old man." Once, I was sitting in his lap and I started kissing him, starting at the top of his forehead and working my way down so I would get every spot on his face. I could feel the tears around his eyes, and when I stopped for a second he just said quietly, "Don't stop now." In that moment, I realized that we were both hungry for the same things. We were both starved for affection and needed to be appreciated and accepted for who we really are. And we both wanted our mutual love to be complete and unconditional.

After our incredible time together Jud had to return to his sub-marine, and I went back to school in Santa Barbara to finish my last quarter and graduate. Our plan was that right after I graduated from the university I would meet up with the navy wives and fly with them to the Far East in order to follow the submarine WestPac tour. Our first port of call was in Japan.. Then we would continue on to Taiwan and Hong Kong, following the route of his boat so that we could meet up at each port. It sounded like such a won-derful adventure, but mostly I was just looking forward to seeing Jud again.

In the meantime, I was a bridesmaid at Sandy's wedding on November 28, 1970. I had a chance to spend some more time with Jean, my future mother-in-law, and we bonded even more. She helped me choose my own wedding dress, which I found in the very first bridal store we went to. It was the very first dress I tried on! I still remember feeling so excited and proud when I walked out to show her my dress.

It was such a crazy time for me. I was still working three jobs, while simultaneously finishing up with school and planning our wedding. I took my last final in early January, and two days later I was on my way to Japan to see Jud again. I was very ready to leave behind Santa Barbara and my university years. The very last thing I had to do was close my bank account at the local Bank of America. While I was standing in line I had a strange feeling that someone was watching me. I turned around and Hormuz was standing right behind me. I was startled for a moment, thinking that he might have been following me, and I just wanted to get away from him. We did talk very politely for a few minutes, and I wished him well. Then I got out of there as fast as I could!

As I was driving away from campus with all my belongings, listening to music on my favorite radio station, I started crying. So much had happened in the past four years, and I knew it had to be some higher power who had brought Jud into my life. Even in my loneliest moments God never forgot about me, though sometimes I hadn't been sure about that, and now I simply needed to follow the path He had provided for me.

Jud made all the arrangements for my trip to the Far East, and while I was excited to see him, I was also bone-tired from work, studying for finals, and packing and moving out of Santa Barbara. I was going on less than four hours' sleep a night for several weeks. Still, I couldn't sleep on the plane and felt that I might be getting sick. The flight was very long, but all I kept thinking about was that soon I would be in Jud's arms and everything would be fine.

The plane finally landed in Sasebo, Japan, and there was Jud, waiting for me with open arms as always. Unfortunately, the first couple of days I *was* pretty sick, and I couldn't keep anything down. Jud was very loving and patient, and after a few days I started to feel like my old self again. In Sasebo we stayed in a traditional Japanese hotel, and it was very romantic. We took a traditional Japanese bath and had a very special Japanese dinner prepared just for the two of us. We slept on the floor on a very comfortable and soft tatami mat.

Jud already knew so much about the local history and culture, and he was a great tour guide. One day we took a train to Fukuoka to see some sights, and during the ride we talked a lot about our upcoming wedding. I told him that I would rather elope because my preference would be that both of my real parents attend our wedding and since that was not possible I would rather not have an actual ceremony. I still held on to my childish dream of seeing my mother and father together just once, even though they were both married to other people. I still hadn't let go of my unrealistic notion that my mother and father could still love each other after all these years.

I was full conflicting emotions. One minute I was happy beyond words and then I panicked, wondering whether I was doing the right thing. What if this marriage didn't work out and we had children? Would I put them through the same misery I experienced? What if Jud didn't love me anymore and fell for someone else? I remember how I tried to explain to Jud all the reasons why I didn't think marriages ever worked out. I said that even if everything was

great during the courtship, once the marriage was official, everything changed. That was the only kind of marriage I knew. I said
that many couples stay together but still cheat on each other or are
miserable in their relationship. Jud's parents were a perfect example!

Of course, Jud always had a way with words. He explained to
me that the wedding ceremony was not just for us, but also to
honor our parents and for our families and to make our union official. He kept reassuring me how much he loved me, and saying
that after we were married our love would grow and be even
stronger. The only time I could let go of my anxiety was when we
made love. For those moments I could let go of all my fears and believe that our love was so real that nothing could ever change us.

After one week in Japan, the submarine left for the next port.
The wives and I flew together to our next stop, Taipei, the capital
of Taiwan. We stayed in a pretty nice hotel downtown, but it was
a very depressing city with a lot of poverty all around us. I never
felt comfortable there and couldn't wait to leave. Then I ran into a
problem when it was time for me to go on to Hong Kong. I had
given up my Hungarian citizenship years before but hadn't yet
taken the oath to become an American citizen. My passport said
"Stateless," and that created some suspicion with the Chinese con-
sular staff. Jud was by my side with all my documents, but they
wouldn't allow me to leave Taipei until they did further checking
into my background. The submarine and all the wives left, and I
had to stay behind. Jud and I agreed that if I could not get out of
Taiwan, he would fly back to Taipei so we could spend his remaining few days of leave together.

I spent two whole days sitting in the waiting room of the con-
sulate before they finally let me go. I was completely alone and
spoke to no one other than the consul and his receptionist. The
evenings were the scariest because the hotel was dark, so I just
stayed in my room. On each floor of the hotel there was an atten-
dant who sat in the corner watching people coming and going
around the clock, expressionless. I never saw him speak to anyone—in fact I barely saw him move away from his post. I did not

trust him at all, and I made sure that my door was locked tightly at night.

Then, without any real explanation, I was given the green light to leave for Hong Kong. Thankfully, I arrived there the night before the submarine was getting into port. I connected with the wives right away, and we planned to take the ferry the next morning to the Kowloon side to meet our significant others at the ferry terminal. It was a very long day, and Jud and I kept missing each other; but finally we reunited by midnight. We were both exhausted but very happy I had been able to get out of Taiwan safely. I could tell Jud was looking forward to our special few days in Hong Kong.

Jud had been saving most of his navy pay so we could buy many things we would need as a married couple. I will never forget when he took out an envelope with eleven hundred dollars—all in twenty-dollar dollar bills—and said that this was the place where we should spend all the money and get everything we needed. Eleven hundred dollars was a lot of money in 1970, and the dollar bought a lot more in Hong Kong. Jud told me that we could have custom-made clothes made here very inexpensively.

What I wanted more than anything were shoes. I had never had enough of them as a kid, and I always dreamed about having nice-fitting shoes without holes in the soles. When I told Jud why I wanted to buy shoes, he said the sweetest thing. "Once we are married you can buy all the shoes you want!" I am sure he regretted having said that many times over the years, but he did keep his word!

Hong Kong was amazing! I loved everything about that bustling city. The Victoria Hotel was beautiful, and our time there was unforgettable. This was where Jud surprised me and told me he would pay for my mother and stepfather to travel from Hungary so they could attend our wedding and share in our special day. I was elated. My parents were going to see each other for the first time in sixteen years and be there to witness our wedding!

Jud was really my knight in shining armor. Everything he did for me and everything he said to me were things I used to read about in romance novels. I simply couldn't believe anyone could love me the way he did. I was still apprehensive that it might not last, but I let go of my resistance and opened up my heart completely to him.

Hilo Airport, on the Big Island of Hawaii right after my arrival.

Jud took this picture when I was lost in thought admiring the
breathtaking beauty of this island.

Chapter 16
OUR BIG DAY

We decided to get married on the naval base on Treasure Island because the setting—in the center of San Francisco Bay, overlooking the city San Francisco, Marin County, Berkeley, and Oakland—was so beautiful. There was a chapel right on the base and an officer's club for the reception. It was affordable and a great location for our guests.

We agreed on a double ceremony, with both a rabbi and a minister to honor my father's Jewish faith as well as Jud's Episcopal faith. We decided the minister would officiate during the marriage vows, but the rabbi would do the speaking part (I always had a soft spot for rabbis because they were usually wonderful speakers). The rabbi asked us if we wanted him to write something in advance or just speak impromptu. I told him that after the traditional breaking of the glass we just wanted him to say whatever he was inspired to say when he looked at us. I was sure he would do a great job.

A couple of months before our wedding, I woke up to go for my morning run and felt an excruciating pain in my left knee. I consulted several doctors, but they couldn't find anything wrong with my knee. Could this have been from my constant anxiety and fear of getting married? I was really struggling, but just kept going.

Two weeks before the big day, Jud arrived. Jean, my soon-to-be mother-in-law, planned a surprise wedding shower for us (which was great because we had nothing except for the things we had purchased in Japan and Hong Kong). I didn't even know what a wedding shower was! I was told only that we were going to visit some friends for an afternoon tea. I was deeply touched because it was planned so I could share this special event with Jud, and it gave me a chance to meet many of his family's friends. Of course, he was in on the surprise. Even though I had never met any of these people before, I could tell they were all there for Jud and wanted to be a part of this special moment in his life. They were, of course, curious to meet me as well. It was a bit overwhelming for me, as I was more used to doing things for others. It was hard for me to accept when people did things for me. What made me the most happy, though, was seeing how much everyone loved my future husband.

Five days before our wedding, my mother and Gyula arrived. Jud and I picked them up at the airport and took them to his parents' home. I was anxious and excited about this moment, but Jud was wonderful as always and made my mother and Gyula feel completely welcome. We did a bit of sightseeing, but my mind was elsewhere. All I could think about was what would happen when my mother and father faced each other for the first time after so many years. The last time they saw each other was during the revolution in 1956, when my father picked me up to go to the country for "food and supplies," when he was secretly planning our escape from Hungary. Occasionally over the years my mother would bring up this subject. She was very angry that he would have taken me away without her knowledge. But it had been sixteen years, so I was hoping their meeting would be a happy event.

When my father, Irma, and the boys arrived the next day, I was shaking from nerves, but the evening went well and my parents were very cordial to each other. Gyula liked and respected my father a great deal, and they seemed to enjoy sharing stories about life in Hungary before the revolution. Irma and my mother got along fine as well. My parents seemed friendly toward each other, and their conversation focused mostly on how pleased they were that I was marrying such a great young man. My childhood dream of seeing both my father and mother in the same room sharing in my happiness came true. I knew they were proud of me. I was beyond grateful to Jud for making this day so special for me, and the love I felt for him was overwhelming.

Unfortunately, though, my leg kept getting worse, and I was full of anxiety as I thought about the whole idea of marriage. When I looked at Jud and saw him so happy and so sure of himself, I would feel better for a moment, but then at night I would be full of doubts again. I wondered if I would get through the rehearsal that evening at the chapel because I would have to walk up some steps. I was in a lot of pain. My father told me to hold on to him, and he would help me down the aisle. The four steps I had to walk up to the altar were the hardest. I tried to walk slowly so my slight limp wouldn't be noticeable. (My brother-in-law, Craig, joked about all the fun we would have on our honeymoon if I could barely move my legs!) Oddly, Jud's father missed the rehearsal dinner and didn't show up until late that night. I don't think he wanted to be there. It seemed he didn't like to see his son happy. Jud wasn't particularly surprised, and knowing how antisocial his father was—especially around people he didn't know—actually made the evening much more pleasant for everyone.

After dinner, Jud left for the night so that—according to tradition—we wouldn't see each other until our actual ceremony. My father, Irma, and the boys went to their hotel, and my mother and Gyula stayed with me at Jud's parents' house. Gyula slept in Jud's room, and my mother and I were in Sandy's old room. Neither of us slept a wink that night. We talked about the past, and my mother tried to explain why she hadn't been the mother I deserved. Once again she told me that she was "not cut out to be a mother" and probably would have been better off never having children. She probably thought this would make me feel better about our past, but in truth it never did. She said she felt a lot of guilt after I left for America. Even though she wanted to make up for the past, she felt that God had taken me away from her permanently and that was her punishment. Anyway, I told her that I understood and knew she did the best she could.

I did ask her a few questions about her second marriage, because I was curious how she could have kept going back to the man who had caused her to lose everything she had. She said she simply couldn't say no to him. By the time she found out he had a gambling addiction, they were already married and he was controlling her completely. She said she felt bad about those years because she lost touch with her entire family, including me, and was afraid she had lost me for good. She added that she thought my leaving for America and choosing my father over her was her punishment for that time. We both cried, and I kept reassuring her that I loved her very much and that my special day wouldn't have been special if she hadn't been with me. I said that if she and Gyula had not been there, we would not have had the ceremony at all. I think this helped her calm down and made her feel much better about the day ahead of us. By God's grace and guidance, everything turned out fine.

The morning of our wedding day—Saturday, March 21, 1971— Sandee drove me to Treasure Island early to get ready. It was a gorgeous San Francisco spring day, with a cool breeze and the sun shining brightly. We shared such a special time on our drive, and I was hoping that that we would grow even closer over time. I wore Sandee's veil as my "something borrowed" item, and she shared a little bit about her first four months of marriage. She seemed very happy and in love. I was still full of conflicting emotions regarding the idea of marriage. The only thing I was sure of was that I loved Jud, and no one had ever come even close to making me feel the way he did.

Everyone treated me so wonderfully on the day of our wedding that I felt like a princess. It seemed as if I just floated through the day, with everything happening very fast. Before I could even catch my breath, the time had come to walk down the aisle and pledge my life to Jud. My leg was still hurting when my father came to get me and whispered, "just hold on to me and you will be fine."

When I walked into the chapel with Dad, all I saw was Jud with the most radiant smile on his face. His smile was like a magnet, and I just fixed my eyes on him. I felt safe. In that moment, everything was right with the world and all my anxieties vanished. I was in such a dream state that it felt like an out-of-body experience. I felt vindicated and free of the past. It was moving to see my mother and father both witnessing this sacred moment. I guess sometimes dreams do come true—maybe not exactly the way we want or expect, but God does listen to our prayers. I was beyond grateful to

God and to Jud for making my dreams become reality.

After the official part of the ceremony was over, it was the rabbi's turn to speak. At first it seemed he had nothing prepared, but then he looked at us intently and took our hands. This is what he said: "On this day it is traditional to wish you both long life and much happiness, but I choose to wish you something else instead. I wish for you that there should never be a day in your lives when you think you know each other well enough not to explore any further. Every day should be a new day. When you wake up each morning, say to yourself, 'He/she is a stranger and I don't know him/her, so God, please, help me to love him/her for today.' Your love should be for both today and the rest of your lives." Then he gave us the traditional Jewish blessing and we were husband and wife. His words guided our marriage for over four decades.

After the ceremony and photographs, it was time for the reception. I hardly remember any of it, because everything happened very quickly and continued to feel like dream to me the whole time. Before I had a chance to enjoy the moment it was time to change and leave for dinner in Sausalito and then go on to Tiburon, where we were going to stay at a charming hotel for our first married night.

When I was changing in to the "going-away" dress I had picked out for our special night, Jean came in to help. I hugged her and called her Mom for the first time. Then she said, "There is something I need to ask you, honey." I looked at her seriously and said, "Anything, Mom. What is it?" She was quiet for a moment, and then she said, "You know I tried to do the best I could to raise Jud, but I failed in one important thing. I didn't really praise him enough while he was growing up, and of course Jerry never did. He was always jealous of Jud, and when the girls were born he became even more resentful of him. I just tried to keep everything on an even keel. I should have let Jud know how proud I was of him, but I was afraid his dad would become even more difficult. Don't forget to praise Jud and always let him know when you are proud of him!" I hugged her and said, "Praising Jud should be an easy task, because he is a very special man and I love him with all my heart." I have kept my promise to Jean, my wonderful mother-in-law, for forty-four years and going strong.

We said our good-byes, and then Jud and I were off in our get-away car, which was decorated with colorful flowers. Our dinner was beautiful and very romantic, in a restaurant in Sausalito over-looking the Bay, and then we were off to our little hotel in Tiburon.

For a brief moment I tried to imagine my mother and father being together on their wedding night, in love with each other. What happened to those feelings, and when and how did they stop? How does one make love last? I just pushed those thoughts out of my head and cherished the moment.

When we walked into our room, Jud carried me over the doorstep, and I could not believe my eyes. There were red rose petals everywhere, all the way to our bed! After that I don't re-member much.

When we woke up the next morning, my husband smiled at me and asked, "And how is your leg?" The pain was completely gone. Was the pain in my leg caused by my irrational fear of being mar-ried? I will never know for sure; but I do know that in that mo-ment, waking up in the morning with Jud's arm around me, I felt only joy, love, and a sense of belonging that I have never felt be-fore.

We spent Sunday opening presents at Jud's parents' home, and then flew to Hawaii for our honeymoon. Our final destination was Kauai, but we stopped in Honolulu to meet with Jud's captain and the rest of the officers and their wives. I had met them before dur-ing our trip to Asia, but this time was different. I was now Jud's wife, and they came to welcome me to my new navy family.

Our honeymoon was wonderful, but much too short. It rained almost the entire week; but we didn't mind. We were either touring the island, walking in the warm tropical rain, or making love. I do recall one night waking up in a panic. I kept repeating to myself, "I am a married woman!" What did that really mean? What should I do so our love would last a lifetime? I was still insecure and afraid that I would disappoint Jud. Eventually I drifted off to sleep and felt better the next day. We toured the entire island, and the beauty of Kauai took my breath away. We fell completely in love with the island, and it has remained our favorite spot on the planet to this day.

On the last day of our honeymoon the sun finally came out, so of course we were trying to get a suntan. That was a big mistake. We burned so badly that on our last night together we could barely touch, and even lying on our sheets was painful! We were both a little sad when we got on the plane to head back to Honolulu and to the little apartment in Waikiki that Jud had rented for us.

I tried very hard not to think about the fact that Jud was going to sea for three weeks for military exercises and I would be by myself in our apartment, not knowing anyone or how to get around the island. I had never even driven Jud's car before, so it would be a lot of new things all at once. Jud assured me that I really couldn't get lost in Hawaii, because the islands are so small that you just go around and make a big circle.

Our apartment was sparsely furnished, and since our navy shipment had not arrived we had basically nothing except the things we carried in our suitcases. On our first night there, Jud got a bottle of Champagne to celebrate being in our first little home, and we toasted each other using a plastic cup and one of Jud's old coffee mugs!

The next day Jud had to report to the submarine at Pearl Harbor by 7:00 a.m. We drove his Chevelle convertible to the base, and I was trying very hard to remember what route he was taking so I could find my way home. He told me to look for Diamond Head, which was an important landmark and very close to our apartment building. As long as I was going toward it, I wouldn't get lost. We got to the base with no time to spare, and we said our good-byes. I assured Jud that I would be okay, but I cried all the way back to our place, not having any idea what I would do with myself while he was gone. I was hoping that our household shipment would arrive from California with all of our wedding gifts so I could make our apartment more like a home by the time Jud got back from the sea.

We didn't have a television set, but I did have a battery-operated radio that kept me company. I was still an avid runner, so I went for really long runs every morning, and I walked all over Waikiki to get familiar with our neighborhood. I also met our next-door neighbor, a native Hawaiian, who was an enlisted guy in the Navy. He was a cook on one of the ships in Pearl Harbor. He could tell I was pretty lost, and was very kind to me. He told me that I shouldn't be out at night, that the neighborhood was not very safe because of drug dealers and prostitutes. I made sure that I locked my door at night and stayed inside after dark. I found out that our section of Waikiki was called the Jungle because of all the crimes and the police presence around the area. I learned later that Jud didn't have any idea about any of these things when he rented the place.

I spent a lot of time walking on the beach as the days crawled by. I drove around a lot and slowly got to know my way around the island as well as the Pearl Harbor Naval Base. I knew I could have called on some of the other officers' wives, but I was too shy. I had also made it very clear to Jud that I did not want to live in navy housing, mainly because all the houses looked exactly the same. It felt like some sort of institutional living as opposed to private living quarters. I'm not sure why it bothered me so much, but looking back on it today I think it reminded too much of my life under the Communist regime. We all had to look alike and wear the same uniforms, and I was against uniformity of any kind. Later on, as I learned more about the American military and its contribution to the world, my outlook completely changed. I became a serious advocate and supporter of our military!

Three days before Jud was due to return, our shipment finally arrived. I worked around the clock to make everything perfect. I wanted to welcome my husband and make everything really special because he was going to be home only for a few days. I was both exhausted and excited when I got to the base, and I was determined to make the most of our brief weekend together.

I prepared a traditional American dinner: steak, baked potato, salad, apple pie, and, of course, Champagne. Our reunion was very emotional, and Jud was impressed with all I had been able to accomplish in such a short time. (And the wives were correct: when our guys got off the boat, their skin smelled of diesel oil, which made sense since they were on a diesel submarine and couldn't shower every day.) As luck would have it, because of my lack of sleep and all the excitement around his homecoming, the Champagne made me so sick that instead of romance I threw up all night and didn't recover until the next morning. We did make up for it the next day, though, and I was so happy to have my husband home.

I told Jud about all the things I'd learned about the neighborhood, and two months later we moved to a new place that was a lot safer and in a great location: 620 McCully Street, overlooking the Ala Wai Canal. It was our home for the next eighteen months, and to this day I have many special memories about it. I can honestly say it was the first place in my life that I could call home.

We did have our share of ups and downs also. I was still struggling with the whole idea of being married, and with my moodiness I know I tested Jud's patience at the beginning. I think I was scared that I could love someone so much, and I honestly didn't believe that love like this could last. I also didn't particularly care for the navy life at the beginning. I was looking forward to Jud getting out of the military so we could start our civilian life. I tried to be very supportive. We had all Jud's superiors and friends over for dinner parties, and we also attended many military socials.

Dick and Cheri MacDonald were the first couple we had over to our McCully home. Dick was Jud's best friend from high school, who had joined the Navy about the same time. Dick and Cheri were married a couple of years earlier than us and were on their way back to the States from his three-year tour in Japan. They had a layover in Honolulu, and I loved them from the moment we met.

Jud spent a lot of time in the MacDonald home while they were in high school in Sunnyvale, California. Dick's family considered Jud one of their boys. There were five MacDonald brothers, so Jud just blended in with the rest of them. Dick was a great friend, and he knew that Jud's father was not a fan of kids in general. While Dick came over to the Scott home a few times, Jud much preferred to be at Dick's house, where he felt like a member of the family. When Dick and Cheri left, we promised that we would reconnect as soon as we got back to California. Our special bond and friendship has remained strong throughout our lives. To this day they feel more like family than just friends.

At this time, Jud and I started to talk about my becoming an American citizen. This was difficult for me because I still identified myself as Hungarian. When I arrived in America, I was very conflicted in my political views. I was deeply convinced that equality was a good thing, and I grew up in an environment in which we were told what to do, what to say, and what to think in our daily lives. Coming to America and being exposed to so much freedom was hard at first.

As I learned more about American history, I began to understand what freedom of choice really meant. I had to dig deep to find out who I really was, what I wanted to accomplish in my life, and how hard I was prepared to work toward my goals. I finally understood that becoming an American citizen didn't take anything away from my Hungarian roots. It allowed me to participate, to have a voice, and to vote!

Jud taught me by his example what America was all about. He was passionate about always trying to make a difference and always doing more than what was expected of him. I was afraid of losing my roots and my identity, but at the same time I admired my husband's love for his country—and I was also very grateful to be in America. I finally made the decision to become an American citizen.

I had to give up my stateless status and pass a history exam before taking the oath. It was a very touching ceremony when I "pledged allegiance to the flag of the United States of America" along with three hundred other people at the federal courthouse in Honolulu on December 8, 1971. The entire wardroom from Jud's submarine came to celebrate with me on this special day, and it was a very emotional experience. The people who took their oath of allegiance with me that day were my brothers and sisters because we all shared in this special moment. We all dreamed of a brighter future and the many freedoms this great country was willing to give us.

Jud was so proud that I had finally taken this big step. I knew it would bring us even closer together. When the ceremony was over, the entire wardroom was waiting for me outside with flowers and, of course, an American flag. It is a memory I will cherish forever.

Jud decided that after leaving active navy duty, he would go to law school. He spent most of the evenings studying hard to prepare for the upcoming entrance exams. By this time I was quite busy also because had I started working, too. I applied for a sales position at Liberty House, which was one of the finest fashion apparel department stores in Honolulu. They hired me for temporary help during the Christmas season, and I loved every minute of it. At the time I didn't know I had started a career that was to last over forty-five years! I did very well at Liberty House and became their top salesperson the very first month. Our sportswear buyer, Jean Moberly, became my mentor and taught me a lot about the retail business. We remained close friends until her untimely death in the mid-1980s.

Our first year and a half in Hawaii was one of the most memorable and precious times of our married life, but it was also the hardest for me. I was trying to figure out my role as a young wife, friend, and romantic partner to my husband, and often I felt inadequate and insecure. I knew I was testing Jud's patience to the limit. Subconsciously, I think I was trying to prove to him that love didn't last and that eventually he would be unfaithful and leave me.

I think something that made our marriage stronger was our monthly wedding anniversaries. It was Jud's idea that we celebrate our anniversary every month, and it also helped us to recall our rabbi's words to reaffirm our love for each other every day. On the twenty-first day of every month we had a special date when we focused on our love and commitment all over again. Our (nearly) two years in Hawaii were among the most special times in my life, and Hawaii has remained our happy place to this day.

March 20th 1971: Top photo is of my Mother with Irma. Bottom photo is of my Father with Gyula, with me in between them. This was the first time my parents had seen each other since 1956.

March 21, 1971 Our special double wedding ceremony with and
Episcopal Minister and a Reformed Rabbi at the Naval Base Chapel
in Treasure Island, in San Francisco.

Dream Come True; both of my parents present on one of the most special days of my life with their respective spouses.

A sweet old lady took this picture of us on our honeymoon in
Kauai, at the Fern Grotto when they dedicated the Hawaiian
wedding song to us. She just walked up to us and said, "You two
just look so in love; may I take a picture of you?" I was so
touched, and I will never forget her.

My citizenship photo, taken at the
Pearl Harbor naval base.

Chapter 17
CAREER YEARS

After Jud finished his active duty, it was time to move back to the mainland. He was accepted at the University of Santa Clara Law School, and we started a new chapter in our married life. It was very hard for me to leave Hawaii, just when I had finally come to feel comfortable there. Jud assured me that we would go back many times—a promise he has kept all these many years.

The adjustment of moving back to California from Hawaii was hard for me. I was sad for months. Liberty House arranged for my transfer so I could work in the San Jose store, but that shopping center was in a bad area of the town and I never quite felt safe working there. Of course, it didn't help that Jud became completely immersed in law school while I was establishing myself as a junior executive.

We found an apartment—a two-bedroom with a balcony—less than a mile from Jud's school, which worked out great because the owners also hired us as managers of the apartment building. This reduced our rent considerably, and we could make extra money cleaning the apartments when the tenants moved out. We got to know the owners really well, and did such a good job managing the building that we kept it full and there was virtually no turnover during the time we were there.

Jud kept encouraging me to get involved in the law school spouses' organization so I could make more friends and have an easier time adjusting to living in California again. Soon after we moved back to the mainland, Jud surprised me for our second wedding anniversary. He had a white double carnation lei delivered to my office at the store on the day of our anniversary, and then he took me out to dinner at a very romantic restaurant. I was touched beyond words, but it also made me a bit sad that we were not in Hawaii to celebrate.

I started going to the Law Wives Club, which was later changed into the Law School Community Association because we also had a number of husbands whose wives attended law school. Jud encouraged me to run for president of the club, but I couldn't imagine that anyone would consider me for that position. Nevertheless, I finally decided to run for president of the LSCA despite being completely certain that nobody would vote for me. I honestly didn't know what I would be required to do as president of the organization, but I did know that the law students were so immersed in their studies that I wanted their wives and husbands to somehow become a part of this intensive three-year journey.

When election time came, we had to give our speeches in front of all the association members. There were three other people running for president, so I had pretty strong competition. Jud helped me write my speech, but in the end I just spoke from the heart and said what came to my mind. The focus of my speech was how spouses could be supportive of each other during the challenging years of law school. I outlined a plan to invite interesting law professors to our monthly meetings, and I pledged to throw many social events where we could all interact and not feel left out of our spouses' new legal world.

I won by a landslide, and I still remember Jud's face looking at me with such pride! I was in complete shock because I had never been the president of anything and wasn't sure what I was supposed to do. I had a lot of ideas for events that would be fun, but I had to figure out how to execute them. Fortunately, the school year ended and I had the whole summer to learn my new role as the LSCA president.

We also took some courses together on goal-setting and self-improvement. I was very aware that I had some deep-seated problems with my self-image. I had always believed that I should focus only on others to avoid becoming self-centered. It took years to learn that loving myself helped me to love Jud and others more fully as well.

In the summer of 1973, Jud's grandfather gave us some money

so we could take a nice summer vacation. We decided to drive to the Canadian Rockies through Oregon and Washington State to see more of our beautiful country. The trip was unforgettable. It was also the coldest spring in Canada in thirty years! The lakes were still frozen at the end of May, and there was a lot of snow on the ground, especially at the higher elevations. We didn't have winter clothes with us, so we were freezing most of the time. We had planned romantic campouts in different parts of Canada, but ended up staying in hotels where we could warm up and get some good sleep. We drove home via Reno, Nevada, where it was over 100 degrees Fahrenheit, and finally thawed out! Still, it was a wonderful and very memorable trip and I got to see more of our beautiful country in addition to Canada. We drove through Idaho and Nevada on our way home.

On the drive home I prepared for my very first meeting as the president of the LSCA. I had no idea how to conduct a formal meeting. Jud was driving and teaching me parliamentary procedure, helping me step by step. I was pretty nervous at first, but everything turned out well. In fact, our club grew to be the largest one in the law school. I planned some wonderful programs with exciting speakers, and a lot of social events. When my term came to an end, we had a special lunch where I handed over my gavel to the next president. The dean of the law school was our keynote speaker, and he didn't disappoint the audience. He personally thanked my board and recognized my own personal contribution for our successful year. I also spoke and thanked everyone for their participation and support. I was very surprised when the board presented me with a gold necklace with a key and heart attached. It was a very touching moment, and I deeply appreciated their sentiments.

Our marriage also grew stronger, but I still had a long way to go in my personal and professional growth. I slowly began to understand what it meant to accept and love myself, but for some reason it was a struggle for many years before I developed true confidence from within.

Our three years in Santa Clara flew by quickly, and then Jud graduated. I was so proud of him. He was a great student, and he also worked part-time jobs at law firms, was selected for the law review, and participated in numerous extracurricular activities while in school. He clerked one semester for one of state Supreme Court justices, and the experience was invaluable to his career.

I planned a special party for Jud to celebrate his graduation from law school. Our apartment was too small for this affair, so I asked Jean if we could celebrate at their house. She was more than willing to do it, but Jerry would not allow it. I was sad but not surprised. He did not want to be a part of anything that had to do with Jud's accomplishments, even though my father was going to pay for everything. Eventually, one of Jean's close friends offered her home to celebrate this milestone, and my father paid most of the expenses. My father was a very frugal man, but when it had to do with education he was most generous. He was very proud of Jud graduating from law school with high marks.

Our plan was that after Jud took the California bar exam we would take a trip to Hungary. I so wanted him to see my beautiful country and meet and get to know more of my family back home. I wanted to show him the orphanage so he could see where I had spent ten years of my life. I wanted to walk the streets of Budapest with him and wipe away all the memories of when I was walking there alone, often in the middle of the night, looking for my mother. I wanted my extended family to meet the man God had brought into my life, whose love was such an unexpected and wonderful gift. I wanted them to see how my life had turned out despite the odds stacked against me. I was full of anticipation about how the family would receive us. So three days after Jud finished his bar exam, we were on Lufthansa Airlines flying to Hungary. It was August 1975. I was excited beyond words.

We landed in Budapest, exhausted but full of anticipation for our reunion with my family. My mother and Gyula now lived in the suburbs of Budapest. They had bought a very nice house with a big garden and were doing quite well financially. They hired a driver for our visit so we could travel the countryside and show Jud the best of Hungary.

Mom planned several family gatherings, and they were all fun (and pretty emotional). Each dinner was over the top. They certainly gave my husband and me a very special "Hungarian welcome!" I think they were cooking for days in preparation for our visit. I was terrified that if we ate everything that was prepared for us, I would look like the Goodyear Blimp by the time we got back home! My Uncle Imre, who was now a well-known poet in Hungary, hit it off with Jud the minute they met. Imre spoke fairly good English, and that was, of course, very helpful.

I didn't realize how tired Jud had become from preparing for and taking the bar exam, and the day after our very emotional reunion with my mother and Gyula, he caught the flu and ran a high fever. He had to stay in bed for several days, but after the first week he started feeling better so we were able to do some sightseeing. The very first place I took him was the Jewish Orphanage.

I will never forget that day for as long as I live. We took the streetcar and the subway to get there, and I felt very nervous as we were approaching the building. We hadn't called ahead, so I had no idea what to expect. I assumed things would be pretty quiet there because it was the summer and the kids would all be with family or at foster homes. The only people who stayed over the summer were Aunt Olga (since she was the head supervisor and lived there) and some administrative staff who worked in her office.

When we came to the iron gate to the courtyard, the first thing I noticed was that everything seemed much smaller than I remembered. I wondered if Aunt Olga would recognize me, as I was sixty pounds lighter and looked very different from when she saw me last. I had changed a lot during the past twelve years. We walked through the courtyard and came to the big wooden entrance door to the main building. I was so nervous I was shaking when I pushed down the door handle. The door wasn't locked but it was very heavy, so I had to push down really hard. When we walked in, there was Aunt Olga at the top of the staircase, looking down and pushing her glasses up her nose trying to see who these unexpected visitors were.

Her hair was snow-white. Before I knew it, tears were pouring down my face. Finally, I managed to say in Hungarian, "Hello, Aunt Olga." She just stared at me for a moment and then quietly replied, "Ildiko? Is that you?" I ran up the stairs and we hugged for the longest time. She kept repeating over and over: "You are so grown up! You are so beautiful and so thin!" Jud was affected by this emotional scene as well. I was very proud to introduce Jud to her, and I could tell she was pleased with my choice of husband.

Olga invited us into her flat. We had some tea and cookies and shared all the things that had happened to us the past dozen or so years. She spoke a little bit of English, but most of the time I was translating our Hungarian conversation for Jud. He was such a gentleman, as always, and he won Aunt Olga over in the first five minutes. At one point I excused myself to use the bathroom—the same one where I had spent so much time on my knees memorizing poems. I did get on my knees again just for a moment, but this time I just said a quick and quiet thank-you to God for being with me, for guiding me, protecting me, and loving me all these years. My life could have turned out so differently if it had not been for some higher power watching over me.

I observed my former supervisor now as she interacted with Jud. Was this the same person who used to scare me the most? Aunt Olga managed the orphanage with an iron fist, but now she seemed much kinder, and even vulnerable, to me. I took the opportunity to thank her for the beautiful letters she had sent to my father. She smiled and said, "You're welcome, Ildiko. I know I was tough on you, but you never disappointed me. It was very hard managing eighty-five girls with such varied backgrounds. To get results I needed to maintain a disciplined environment." We had a very nice visit, and when we said good-bye I was sad because I would probably never see her again.

Jud and I walked all over Budapest. I showed him my favorite spots and all the places where I used to walk around by myself and dream about the future. It felt surreal as I showed him my favorite bench on Gellert Mountain overlooking the Danube. I took him to the City Park, not far from the orphanage, where we used to march for our May 1 workers parade celebration or the April 4 Independence Day march (when we honored the day the Russians had liberated Hungary from the German occupation). Jud and I walked the streets that used to be my daily route between the school and the orphanage. I wanted him to know and understand me completely. I was deeply touched that he was interested in everything and never once said, "I am tired of this" or "I could use a break" or "I just need a day to rest." He was always willing to do whatever was planned and was fully engaged in all the activities. He even got involved in reading about Hungarian history and tried his best to learn as many Hungarian words and phrases as he could.

We traveled the countryside and visited some of Hungary's most historic cities—Estergom, Eger, Debrecen, Szeged, and Tamasvar—and ate at some amazing restaurants. But the best restaurant of all was my mother's cooking at home. We talked about the possibility of Mom and Gyula coming to America and opening a Hungarian restaurant in California. It was a wonderful thought, but I knew my mother too well. She would be happy running the place for a while, but then she would get tired of it. Mom always lived in the moment, and once she didn't feel like doing something anymore, that was it. I knew you could not run a business in America with that kind of thinking.

The five weeks in Hungary flew by very quickly, and our time there created unforgettable memories. I felt that it brought Jud and me even closer together. Now, when I shared stories of my past, he had a much better understanding because he had met every living member of my mother's family.

I just regret that he never met my precious grandmother, who played such a crucial role in my personal and spiritual development. She was my role model, the kind of woman I wanted to become as an adult. I wanted to love my children the way she loved me. I know she would have been crazy about Jud!

After we got back from Hungary, life became very busy for us. Jud passed the bar exam with flying colors and got his first job at a prestigious law firm in San Francisco's financial district. I was also working in the city, as a junior executive at a well-known specialty store called Joseph Magnin. We were excited about the future.

We bought our first home, east of San Francisco in the city of Walnut Creek. We were somewhat familiar with the area because Jud's grandfather lived nearby in a nice retirement community called Rossmoor. We came to visit him often and had a good feeling about the area. We also liked the local schools, which was very important because we planned to start a family soon. There was an easy rapid transit connection to San Francisco, and we were close to some amazing northern California locales. The Napa-Sonoma wine country was just to the north, the romantic towns of Monterey, Carmel, and Big Sur were just a couple of hours to the south, and Reno and Lake Tahoe were only a few hours east. And right next to us was majestic Mount Diablo, a Bay Area landmark.

Dad, Irma, and the boys used to come up to visit us often while we lived in Walnut Creek. One particular weekend they were there when Jud came home, in uniform, from his Navy Reserve weekend drill. After he greeted my family, he said he was going to change into his civilian clothes, but Dad stopped him and said, "Jud, would you mind not changing your clothes yet? Please, son, just sit down and let me look at you for a little while. I feel so safe when I see an American military man in uniform." So Jud sat down dutifully, and they spent the next few hours just visiting. My father was beaming with pride and looked very happy. He loved America deeply and was grateful for the opportunities this country had given him.

I had learned during our first few years of marriage that my husband was the kind of man who needed to be involved in many community activities, in addition to his demanding work as a trial lawyer. Jud was a born leader, so no matter what organization he joined he usually became its leader very quickly. I had a choice to make: I could either focus solely on my job and not much else, or I could support Jud and involve myself more with his projects. I opted for the latter, and this definitely helped me gain self-confidence. I worked very hard to be successful in my job, but I never thought I was good enough. I always saw myself as inadequate—especially when I compared myself to Jud, who seemed to excel in everything.

During the ninth year of our marriage we were invited by another couple to attend a meeting and learn about a unique program called Marriage Encounter. Apparently, it was designed by a Spanish priest who recognized that there was a lot of information available for those in troubled marriages, but not much for those who wanted to improve basically good marriages. His program was designed to help spouses deepen communication and keep their romantic flame burning bright. This course was considered to be especially helpful for young couples with busy careers, and for couples with children.

Jud decided this was something we should do to grow closer and have a better understanding of each other while we were racing forward in our respective professions. I was very much against it at first because, being in the retail business, I had very few weekends off; the last thing I wanted to do was sit in a room with a bunch of strange couples listening to someone telling us how to have a good marriage. We were very good about celebrating our monthly anniversaries and had always tried to do thoughtful things for each other. I also told Jud that in America there is a "how-to" book for everything. I felt these things were private, and I was not about to share my intimate life with strangers. Nevertheless, Jud signed us up. Eventually I gave in, thinking that he would regret not having listened to me.

To my surprise, it was one of the most special weekends in all our married life. The program weekend we attended was sponsored by a Catholic church, and it was truly a crash course in couples' communication. The weekend began on Friday night with prayer, and then everyone introduced themselves and explained why they had decided to attend the course. Then, even though there were about fifteen or so couples present, the only person we were allowed to speak to for the entire weekend was our spouse.

We were seated in a classroom facing a podium where there was a couple seated with a priest. They talked about the different stages marriages go through and a number of problems that typically arise between couples. They would give us a question, and then we would separate from our spouses to write down our responses. An hour later we would come together and talk about it in the privacy of our room. By Sunday, Jud and I were talking more than we had in the past nine years of our marriage. On Sunday afternoon we were given ninety minutes to write a love letter to each other. The hardest part was when we actually had to read what we had written out loud to each other in the privacy of our room. It was a most intimate and emotional experience for both of us. The weekend culminated when our priest came in and performed a renewal of our wedding vows for the entire group.

We all stood in circle facing one another as we repeated these sacred words of commitment, just as we all had done before on our actual wedding days. It was an incredibly special moment. The words we repeated had so much more meaning this time around, because we now had a shared history. We knew well what each word meant, and we again committed to love, honor, and cherish each other for the rest of our lives. It was so moving.

One of the most important things I learned that weekend was that it is easy to talk about what we think about certain situations in our marriage, but it is very difficult to talk about our feelings. For me, the weekend was a major step in healing the pain from my childhood. Among other things, I learned that I was still very insecure about Jud's love for me. I just never believed I was lovable because of all the rejection I had experienced as a child. When Jud read his love letter to me it was overwhelming because, while I finally began to accept that he truly loved me, I was unsure how to reciprocate his feelings and live up to his expectations. I felt shy and inadequate, and that made it hard to treat him in such a way that he could really feel the depth of my love.

Over time, things got easier as I began to let go of the past and simply trust God's plan. It was time to accept the incredible gift of love my wonderful husband always gave me so willingly. Moving forward, we never missed our monthly anniversaries, and we tried to take a nice two-week vacation every year. Our favorite locale remained the Hawaiian Islands, and we often took shorter trips to Carmel, Mendocino, or Napa Valley to regroup and focus on each other and our relationship.

During these years, Jud worked hard and did very well as a young trial attorney, winning many cases. He continued to be involved in various community groups, and stayed active in the Navy Reserve. We both worked very long hours and had few free weekends together. I had to work almost every Saturday and often on Sunday as well, but I was enjoying wonderful success in my retail career. I worked in various capacities: department manager, store manager, fashion coordinator, and, eventually, as a fashion and wardrobe consultant. During this time, I also worked for three years at a San Francisco television station, dressing and choosing wardrobe for the stars of the show *People Are Talking* on a weekly basis. I was also featured in quarterly fashion segments for the show, which was quite popular at the time. Then I started writing fashion newsletters, and was amazed that within just a few hours I got requests for more than four hundred subscriptions!

While I wanted to have a family, initially I was afraid that Jud might become just like Jerry, that he might not enjoy being a father. I also feared I might become an obsessive mother and ignore my husband in the process. Later, we decided to have children, only to discover that it was not as easy as we assumed. Several years passed without a pregnancy.

One day, when I was preparing for my next TV fashion segment, I got a call from the star of the show. She said, "Ildiko, guess who will be on the show? Dr. Lori Green, the most renowned fertility specialist in the Bay Area. I think you should talk to her after the show. And by the way, she could also use some of your wardrobe tips!" I met Dr. Green the following week and was so impressed by her knowledge and successes with fertility that I told Jud about her. We made an appointment with her shortly thereafter, and I was certain she would be able to help us. Jud liked and trusted her as well, so we decided to work with her. I was now thirty-six years old and Jud was thirty-eight, so in a way it was "now or never" for us.

I was put on very strong fertility drugs and started trying to gain weight so I could carry the baby. The medications made me moody and irritable, but I followed Dr. Green's direction. After the third month of being on a double dosage of medication, I was getting a little depressed. Then I got a call from Jud inviting me to come down to San Diego and join him at the Navy Ball. He was already there for his annual active-duty service in the Navy Reserve, and he wanted me to be there with him. Jud was now a commander, and moving up in the officer ranks. I was definitely not in the mood to party, but I understood that my presence was important to Jud, so I flew down to San Diego to be with him.

After the ball we went back to our hotel, where I fell asleep in Jud's arms. That night I had the most incredible and vivid dream. In my dream I was delivered of the most beautiful baby boy in a San Francisco hospital. I was in a private room with a very sweet nurse, who coached me through an easy delivery. Our little boy looked perfect as I held him in my arms. Jud was sleeping on a cot next to me while I was holding and admiring this precious little child. The nurse came in to check on me and asked, "Mrs. Scott, do you have a name for your little boy so I can make him a wrist tag?" I replied, "Oh, no, everything happened so fast that we never thought of a name . . . but what about Nathan? Is there such a name?" She said, "That is a beautiful name, and if your husband doesn't like it, you can always change it."

During my "Passion for Fashion" career days

ILDIKO SCOTT, Fashion Consultant-Fashion Coordinator, Livingston's, selected a Paul Stanley gabardine suit: jacket, $156; skirt, $80; silk blouse, $64.

❝ Yes, I'm playing it extremely safe, but I selected this piece for its timelessness. I've had an outfit like this for seven years and have just bought another one exactly the same. I still wear the older one for casual wear and the new one for dress. The jacket and skirt can work independently. There are basically five fashion looks — classic, Grace Kelly; romantic, Catherine Deneuve; dramatic, Cher; ingenue, Pia Zadora; sporty, Candice Bergen: With just these pieces I could do infinite variations. ❞

The look of the eighties "Dress for Success" trend.

My handsome Lawyer husband.

One of our many memorable trips to Hawaii during Jud's active duty.

Chapter 18
OUR FAMILY

The dream occurred in March, and I actually did get pregnant in June. Our beautiful little boy came into the world on Wednesday, February 20, 1985. And yes, he was born in San Francisco in a private birthing room, and we named him Nathan Emory Scott! One month after his birth, we celebrated our fifteen-year wedding anniversary. What a special gift he has been!

Three and a half years after Nathan was born, God also blessed us with a little girl we named Lauren Jean Scott. She was our miracle child, because after the birth of Nathan I was told that I would likely not be able to have another child at my age. I was forty-one years old when our beautiful little girl was born. Now our family was complete.

Nathan was just a perfect little boy, and a very easy child to raise. From the beginning I thought he was an old soul. He was sensitive to other people's needs, and was always available to give a helping hand to those in need. I always thought of him as a natural-born leader like his father, and I often wondered what God's plan would be for him. My father was able to be a grandfather to our son for only seven years before his death, but he always told me that Nathan was a very special child and that we should always encourage him to explore his potential.

Nathan was a good student, and was well liked by both his teachers and other kids. He enjoyed his Boy Scout years and went all the way to become an Eagle Scout. He was appointed by the Board of Supervisors as a youth commissioner in our county and was selected to attend a youth leadership conference in Washington, DC. He played all the usual sports, including football, basketball, and swim team, and made many great friends along the way. In his senior year of high school he was the editor in chief of the school newspaper and did a terrific job. In the same year, he also wrote a paper titled "Cowardice and Courage" that was read to the entire senior class. His depth of understanding of the meaning of true courage amazed me, and this was perhaps the first time I had a feeling that at some point Nathan would follow in his father's footsteps and join the military.

After 9/11, he made the decision to join apply for an NROTC scholarship and serve our country. I wasn't happy about it, but at the same time I wasn't surprised. He did his initial NROTC training at the University of Southern California, where he majored in business. After finishing school in four years he decided to become a navy pilot. After successful laser eye surgery to correct his vision to twenty-twenty, he was accepted to the aviation program, and today our son, Lieutenant Nathan (Utah) Scott, is an FA-18 fighter pilot in the United States Navy. He married a beautiful Christian girl, Caitlin (Festian), and they are expecting their first child—and our first grandchild, Caden, as this book goes to press late in the summer of 2015.

Lauren, our miracle child, was so pretty and precocious that it was very difficult not to spoil her. She was also extremely willful and independent, so controlling her was not an easy task. I loved our little girl so much, but she didn't like to be cuddled the way Nathan did as a baby. I was always worried that Lauren wouldn't feel as loved as Nathan, but I could do only as much as she would allow!

She was very active, always on the move. The day she discovered cheerleading and dancing, Lauren was in her element. She participated in cheer and dance all through elementary, middle, and high school.

Dance was Lauren's passion, and that continued even through her college years. The high school years were somewhat challenging, and at times I wasn't sure how we could help Lauren realize her full potential. She always had many friends and, much like her brother, was always the first one to lend a helping hand to a friend in need. It is hard to find a picture of Lauren by herself, because she was always surrounded by a group of friends!

When she went to college at the University of California, Davis,

Lauren blossomed into the most incredible young woman. At that time we noticed many things that told us she would be a great success. While she did fine in school (without much studying), she always had a strong work ethic and always seemed to get raises and promotions in her jobs. Our girl, who always had such a hard time getting ready for school while she lived at home, never missed work and was always on time, regardless how early she had to be up. One week after graduating from college, she had been recruited for a job in San Francisco and was already working while many of her friends couldn't find jobs for a long time. Today she is an account executive at Twitter in San Francisco, and she is well loved by her bosses, coworkers, and clients.

Lauren recently married a wonderful young man she knew from high school, Eric Kiefer. Her wedding was a dream come true, and was a testimony to the kind of loving, thoughtful, and caring person she had become. She continues to have the most wonderful circle of close, loyal friends, and Lauren is the friend they can always count on. We are so very proud of her!

Right after Nathan's birth, I joined the highly regarded specialty store Nordstrom on March 1, 1986. The job came about largely through Jud's support and encouragement. Nordstrom, a Seattle-based company owned by three brothers, had a great reputation of customer service, and when a store was being opened in our area, there were articles written about the company in the local papers. One day Jud turned to me and said, "I think you need to apply and work for this company. Everything you have done in the past is what this company stands for, and I believe it would be a perfect fit!" I just looked at him in complete disbelief. I was finally pregnant with our first child and had a good job (with television exposure!), so I didn't see the need to make any change. My husband had different ideas, though.

Jud put together a complete portfolio of my work with my résumé attached and sent it to Jim Nordstrom, who was the president of the company at the time. I was just smiling to myself, thinking, *I'll never hear from Mr. Jim Nordstrom, and that should put an end to my husband's folly.* Was I ever wrong! Seven days later I received a warm personal letter from Jim Nordstrom. He said he had sent my résumé on to the store manager at the new Nordstrom store in Walnut Creek (where we were still living), and told me they were looking forward to hearing from me as soon as possible.

I was impressed, and eventually joined this great company. My years as a wardrobe consultant, personal stylist, and designer sales manager really paid off. I continued to be a personal shopper and stylist and had the opportunity to hire and manage several teams of stylists. I trained them to be the best in the business, representing and enhancing Nordstrom's service reputation. I worked with some famous designers, traveled all over the country, and helped open many new Nordstrom stores.

The very best part of my job was that I could help people feel good about themselves while discovering both their inner and their outer beauty. I was very aware that from my orphanage years on I had always had a strong desire to be needed, and this was the key that made my job so rewarding and fun. I'll never forget the response when I asked my first store manager and mentor, John Whittaker, "What words of wisdom can you give me that will help me to be successful at Nordstrom?" He said, "Ildiko, I don't want you to worry too much about sales. Just put a big smile on your face and take care of everyone who walks through our door to the best of your ability. Then thank them from your heart for allowing you to take care of them!" His favorite saying was, "Just go out there and embrace the world every day, and you will be successful."

I repeated those words hundreds of times to the many people I trained and worked with all these years, and they served us all well. I won numerous awards and received much recognition for my contribution to Nordstrom, and I am very proud of my twenty-nine-year career with them. The greatest rewards for me were the lifelong friendships and the people I was able to help along the way. My work at Nordstrom was not just a job—it was my passion, my hobby, and a way to give back for all the wonderful things that have happened to me in America. The greatest gift this company gave me was that I was allowed to love and take care of so many people on many different levels, and it also made me want to be a better person in every aspect of my life.

The years flew by so fast. Jud, after being a partner in two law firms, opened his own successful legal practice in Pleasanton in 1988. He also served as president of the county Bar Association, and served at local, state, and national levels of this legal organization. He also donated a lot of time to helping or leading several local community and charitable organizations. He continued to be active in the Navy Reserve and retired as a rear-admiral from the United States Navy Submarine Force in 2001.

Jud closed his law practice in 2009 to accept appointment as a federal administrative law judge. He continues to be active in several community groups and military organizations and has taken a leadership role in the one of the conferences of the judicial division of the American Bar Association, along with several other ABA organizations. He is also very active in our church and leads several men's Christian groups. No matter what my husband becomes involved in, he always seems to be selected for a leadership role. He is my hero, the love of my life, my soul mate, and my very best friend!

Our Family today taken in Princeville Kauai during our summer
vacation of 2014; "Dreams do come True" Nathan, his wife
Caitlin, me, Jud, Lauren and her husband, Eric.

Chapter 19
FAITH AND HOPE

Looking back on my life, I honestly don't know where I would have ended up if I hadn't had my faith and inner guidance to get me through the tough times. It took me many years to find my own truth because I had been exposed to everything from the Orthodox Jewish religion to strict Roman Catholic theology and everything in between. According to the Jewish religion, one's faith/race is carried through the mother. Since my grandmother was of Jewish descent, all her children would be considered the same according to the Orthodox view. But after my grandmother converted to Catholicism, all of her children were baptized and grew up in the Christian church, following the teachings of Jesus. My grandmother was deeply religious, and she remained a faithful follower of Christ throughout her life, even while she was an involuntary trance medium for Christian spirits during séances.

I remember two very special Christmases with my parents while they were still married. In those days I always prayed to Jesus, who was alive and completely real to me, so that I could always talk to him and believed that he heard me. My father never objected to my going to church with my grandmother or my evening prayers to Jesus. In fact, while my mother and father were married, we didn't celebrate any of the Jewish holidays, only the Christian ones. After the Holocaust, my father completely closed the door on his Jewish faith, and I assume that he went along with the Christmas celebrations simply to please my mother.

Everything changed when I moved into the Jewish orphanage at age six. We had religious instruction every Wednesday, where we celebrated and learned about the history of the Jewish people. We studied the Old Testament, but Jesus' name was never mentioned. Our teacher was a wonderful storyteller, and I loved listening to her tell the Creation story and talk about the lives of the Patriarchs like Abraham, Isaac, and Jacob. Moses was my favorite of them all.

At times in school we were bullied and yelled at by other kids for being Jewish and for "killing Jesus." I used to go to bed at night crying bitterly because as a young child I didn't understand what they were talking about. To make things even more confusing, in our schools God was not mentioned at all. In fact, we were told time and again that there was no God. We needed to believe in the Communist Party because it was the only institution that would take care of us and improve our lives. Of course, many of the people who preached to us about the power of the Communist Party and its great leadership could often be found in churches and temples on weekends. We were brainwashed as children, and we never questioned anything. We simply accepted what we were told.

Christmas and Easter were among the hardest times for me. I missed being with family celebrating the birth of Jesus, His sacrifice on the cross, and, most of all, His resurrection. Often I would sneak into any church I could find so I could pray. I always asked for the same things. I prayed to God to keep me safe and pure, and for my mother and father to love me and bring me home. After my father left for America, I prayed to God to help me to reunite with him. I prayed that my mother would stop sleeping with so many different men and would want to take care of me. And I prayed to God to keep her safe when she was in prison. I always ended with the same prayer: I asked God to forgive me for making up stories about why my mother could never come and see me. I didn't want people to think badly of her, and I was embarrassed about what had happened to my own mother.

During those orphanage years I stopped praying to Jesus, but I never stopped praying to God. The Jewish people believe deeply in God and try to live by the Ten Commandments that God gave to Moses at Mount Sinai. The one thing that was consistent in my childhood was that I always had a strong feeling or intuition that there was a guardian angel watching over me. I knew that somehow I would be okay as long as I stayed true to myself. How else could I explain that no one tried to hurt me on the many nights I walked around Budapest looking for my mother? How else could I explain the incident when, while running an errand for my supervisor, I had an uncontrollable urge to take a detour and check on my mother and found her rolling on the bed in an ice-cold apartment in the middle of winter, in severe pain? Had I not have followed my intuition to go home, she could have died.

I could write a separate book including all the examples of how my guardian angel stood by me and protected me under so many challenging circumstances. Throughout most of my childhood there was always someone who would believe in me and help me through the times when there was no family or a friend around. Even at the orphanage, where I had such a hard time fitting in, I met my lifelong best friend, Bea. I often wondered why I was chosen to be the only person to perform at major fund-raisers. How was it that I always had a teacher who would take a particular interest in me and make me feel special when I needed it the most?

Who was the voice who spoke to me in the middle of the night in 1962 and urged me to write a letter to the premier of Hungary asking to be allowed to immigrate to America? How did it happen that my best friend had the very next appointment at the immigration bureau right after me?

My five-year courtship with my husband, Jud, was full of moments when I knew that God had a master plan And no matter how much I tried to control my own destiny, God had other ideas. My guardian angel had to work very hard to keep me on the right path so I would recognize my soul mate, have a wonderful marriage, and learn to love and be loved in return.

During my early years in America, I didn't go to church or to Jewish temple. I had a few discussions with my father regarding his beliefs, but he told me his faith had died with the loss of his family during the war. His words were exactly this: "If God could allow what the Germans did to the Jews during World War II, then there is no God for me." At university I went through an existentialist phase when I decided that everything was relative and our thoughts were our realities. But even during those crazy years, I never stopped praying to God.

After the birth of our son, Nathan, my husband decided that it was time to find a church and raise our children in the Christian faith. At first we didn't share this decision with my father, who was raising my half-brothers in the Jewish faith. The youngest, Ed, felt the Lord's calling and moved to Israel for six months, where he attended a rabbinic school in Jerusalem for a few months to learn more about Judaism and then decided to live his life following the strict Orthodox Jewish tradition. While he was there, he invited my father and Irma to come for a visit. I'll always cherish that special phone call I received from Ed, when they all went to the Wailing Wall. He said, "Ildiko, you will not believe what I am witnessing right now! Our father is singing, dancing with the rabbis, even crying a little." That was where my father prayed for the first time since the loss of his family, and he seemed fulfilled and happy. Ed said it was a sight to behold.

On December 17, 1989, my father died in a freak accident. He fell off a retaining wall onto his head when he was helping his gardener prune a large tree branch at one of his properties. It was exactly thirty-three years from the day of his arrival to America, and three weeks after coming home from the Holy Land. His death was a complete shock, but at least I had the joy of knowing that he knew God again before he passed. I remember thinking at that time that one day I would also go to the Holy Land and pray in the same place where he found his faith again, hoping to find mine.

More than four hundred people attended his funeral, and everyone had something kind to say or a special story to share with me. Dad really loved America and wanted to make people feel welcome all the time. One neighbor came up to me at the funeral and said, "We had just moved into the neighborhood and were in the process of unpacking when this nice one-armed gentleman came to our door with a lovely welcome cake in his hand. He smiled at us and said, 'I just wanted to come over to introduce myself and welcome you to our community. This country has been so good to me, and this is just my way of saying thank you.' We chatted for a few minutes, and he met our two youngsters. After he left, my husband looked at me and said, 'I think we are really going to like it here.' We will never forget Mr. Kalman."

I was always relieved and happy that my father's second wife, Irma, and I had a good relationship. I think I showed over and over that I was forever grateful for all her help when I came to America. In turn, I tried to be the best big sister to my brothers, and I always tried to be available, even after I got married. When my beloved father passed away so unexpectedly, I wanted to be there for Irma in every possible way. I also wanted our children to have a grandmother who was close by to help keep my father's memory alive.

After Dad's funeral, we also planned a private gathering to place his gravestone after it was completed. After the ceremony, I thought we would spend some time with Irma and the boys, but instead something completely unexpected happened. Irma addressed us and said, "The only person who held us together was your father. Now that he is dead, there is no longer any reason for us to have further contact. Good-bye." She turned around and left, never looking back!

We stood there in complete shock and then returned home immediately. At first I could not even cry. But then the tears came, and the feeling of rejection was crushing. I just kept thinking that for so many years she must have barely tolerated my presence while I dared to hope that she might have liked me a little. My only consolation was that I was not the only one. Irma severed her relationships almost all of the friends who had been part of the social circle she shared with my father. I never saw her again. It took me a long time to get over that.

Rob and Ed both took our father's death very hard. Rob had worked tirelessly to make Dad proud, graduating at the top his class at the University of California, Berkeley, and earning a doctorate in engineering at Stanford. Rob doesn't believe in God or follow the Jewish faith, but he's become an extremely successful entrepreneur and businessman. He is brilliant, funny, and very engaging (though there are certain subjects we don't talk about). He's married to a very special woman, LuAnn, and they live south of San Francisco in Portola Valley. Ed is also married and now lives on the East Coast, in New Jersey. He and his wife, Alison, have two boys, Jeremy and Zachary, and they follow the strict Orthodox Jewish tradition. I don't get to see them very often, but knowing about Ed's deep faith in God makes me very happy.

In July 1991 we went back to Hungary. Mom was feeling too ill to meet us at the airport, so Gyula arranged a ride for us. When we got to their place, Mom was sitting in the garden waiting for us. She had lost a lot of weight and was really showing her age, but she lit up when she saw us. We were home for about three weeks and had a wonderful time. It warmed my heart to see Mom with our children. She loved them.

During the last week of our vacation, a voice startled me in the middle of the night, just like in the past. The male voice said, "Have a family photo taken while you are here." The next morning I told Mom that we needed to arrange a family photo. She thought it would be difficult to get an appointment so quickly, but Gyula made it happen, and we got some wonderful pictures taken that still hang in our home today. Little did I know that this was going to be the last time I would see my mother while she still looked like herself.

At the end of August that same year, I received an urgent letter from Mom letting me know that she was not well. She asked me to come back to Hungary immediately in the event she did not make it through surgery. She didn't say outright, but I knew right away she had cancer. I tried not to panic and just pray for her. I knew this was very serious.

Jud made arrangements immediately for me to go home. I got there three days before her surgery, and by this time Mom had lost even more weight. She seemed excited about being slimmer, and I kept telling myself that she would be fine, but I was worried. The entire family gathered around and stayed at the hospital during her surgery.

I spoke with the Oncology Department head, and he said that after this procedure we would know her prognosis. At that time my uncle Imre was the assistant secretary of state for Hungary, so thankfully Mom was getting very good care. I offered to pay the surgeon in dollars if necessary.

The process only took an hour. As I feared, Mom had pancreatic cancer and the prognosis was that she had six months to a year to live at best. I stayed with her for the next two weeks, and then I had to fly home to my family. I stayed in touch with her weekly, and for a time she was doing okay. They were giving her a lot of medication for her pain.

Soon it was Christmas, and between my hectic work schedule at Nordstrom, having two young (and very busy) children, plus a husband with a growing law practice, life was intense. But one night about two weeks before Christmas, I woke up in the middle of the night, and there was that familiar voice again. "Go, be with your mother now!"

I panicked. How would I get off work? How could I do this without spoiling Christmas for our children? How could we afford a trip when flights were at their most expensive?

Jud was, as always, very supportive, and he said we would find a way. In church the following Sunday, I was praying (mostly crying) for my mother. I knew she wouldn't be with us much longer. I kept wondering how we could all be with her in her time of need.

Sitting in the pew, I was deep into my prayers when I felt a tap on my shoulder. I turned and recognized a nice gentleman whom I sort of knew from our church, and he just happened to be a vice-president for a Swiss airline. He asked me very gently, "What's wrong? Can I do anything to help?" I was a mess, so Jud explained our predicament to him. He smiled and said, "Do you have twelve hundred dollars for four round-trip tickets from San Francisco to Budapest?" We said, "Yes, of course!" He said, "Call my secretary tomorrow at 9:00 a.m. and I will have your tickets ready to go. Whatever date works best for you will be fine."

I was grateful beyond words. Because of God's grace and this wonderful man's generosity, we left for Budapest on Christmas Day, 1991 and returned home on January 10, 1992.

My Hungarian family prepared us that we might not recognize my mother at this point. We were afraid the children might have a difficult time seeing her. Mom had a nurse who came in daily to check on her, and my aunt Mandi stayed with her full-time. She was a widow and had become close with Mom in their elder years.

I spent all of my time with Mom. I did everything for her, with the exception of bathing her. She was skin and bones, except for her swollen abdomen from the cancer and fluids, and I simply couldn't bear to see her like that. It reminded me too much of pictures I had seen of people in the concentration camps. We spent the evenings talking and making plans to come back again in the spring. We all wanted to believe that she would still be with us then.

Jud encouraged me to sit down with my mother and tell her that I forgave her for the past, but I simply could not do it. First of all, I was always there for her when she needed me. And at this stage, I did not want her to be reminded of our sad past history. Instead, I wanted only to love her while she was still here.

We returned home on January 10, and mother passed away ten days later, on January 20, 1992. I went through a period of depression for about a year before I started coming back to my happy self. After all, I had so much to be thankful for.

Back in 1988 we had joined an Episcopal church in our neighborhood, but I was questioning everything about Jesus, and I never felt that I really fitted in with that Episcopal church. Then one day years later, everything changed. My guardian angel must have been working overtime. I was invited to join a church's women's Bible study group. Only a few weeks later we were asked if Jud and I could join a small group from that church to go on a trip to the Holy Land. I told them I would talk to Jud and hoped we could make it happen! Here was my opportunity to go to the Wailing Wall and fulfill a promise I had made after I learned what a special place it had been for my father.

Jud was excited about the trip. I knew he wanted to do whatever he could to help me find my truth and heal from the past. Since he was a navy flag officer (an officer above the rank of captain), he had to get military clearance, but everything fell into place and we flew to Israel in April 2000, just a couple of weeks before Easter. I was worried about leaving our children home for twelve days, but my mother-in-law, Jean, came to our aid. As long as our children were with family, especially my wonderful mother-in-law, I knew everything would be okay. I felt in my heart that this trip was supposed to happen.

Our pilgrimage to the Holy Land was everything I had hoped for and more. We visited all the holy sites where Jesus had walked and preached, and we read from the Bible and sang hymns at each stopping point. We had wonderful talks during our evening dinners and shared a lot about our faith. My friend Chris said to me more than once that at some point you just have to accept your faith and stop questioning. Every night when I went to sleep, I asked God what was holding me back when everything I had experienced proved how real Jesus was! I wanted Jesus to be as real to me as he had been when I was a little girl. I wanted to talk to him again the way I had then.

Then I realized that the only thing holding me back was my fear of disappointing my father by "abandoning" my Jewish heritage. I didn't realize this until we went to visit the Wailing Wall, where my father had stood and found God again three weeks before he died.

I was both nervous and excited to go to this holy place. I wanted to go there and pray for guidance. The lines to get to the Wall were very long, and there were hundreds of people from all over the world waiting just to pray and touch the wall. As according to Orthodox tradition, there were separate lines for women and men. At first I was concerned when I saw how long the lines were, but my wonderful friends said, "Ildiko, take all the time you need. Just get in line and we will wait for you." They knew the story about my father and understood how important it was for me to pray in this special holy place. My heart was pounding as I got closer and closer to the wall. I was praying to God, Jesus, and the Holy Spirit to show me the way through faith.

When I finally got to the wall and touched it, I prayed and asked for a sign to help me feel the presence of Jesus and the Holy Spirit in my heart. My eyes were closed, and suddenly I saw a vision of my beloved father's face with his head tilted, nodding in approval. This was the face I knew so well, with his expression that said I was doing a good job in my cello lessons. Dad always tilted his head and smiled at me as he talked. This vision was so real that I opened my eyes to look at the wall in case he was actually there! In that moment, I felt my father's approval and everything changed in my heart. I accepted Jesus. The feeling was both powerful and overwhelming, and when I finally rejoined my friends I just collapsed in their arms and sobbed.

I have never felt such peace in my heart. It took me a while to come down from that incredibly high spiritual experience. I felt so cleansed and wanted to sing my praises from the mountaintop. If there was any place on Earth where one can feel the power of prayer, the Wailing Wall is that magical place. I was so happy to return home and share my truth with our children.

Both Nathan and Lauren are followers of Jesus, and I am so grateful that they each chose mates who have also have deep faith in the Lord. I know this will guide their hearts and always keep them on the right path.

As the years flew by, I often thought about my best childhood friend, Bea. We moved around a lot and over time we lost touch with each other after I got married especially during the years off being a navy wife and when Jud started law school. But God intervened again and brought us back together in 2005.

We were visiting my half brother, Rob and his wife, Luanne on Christmas Day in the South Bay in Portola Valley. It was on a Saturday, December of 2005. As we were talking, Rob said that he found some pictures of my early school years in Hungary, I might like to have. As I was going thru some of the old pictures, and there was my best friend, Bea in our class picture from seventh grade. I could not stop thinking about her all weekend wondering where would I begin my search to find her and reconnect.

On Monday, December 27th, I was working at home on my computer when our home phone rang at 3:30 in the afternoon. Here is our conversation just as it took place on that memorable day:

"Hello, is this the Scott residence?" I replied:"Yes, it is"

"Is there a gentleman named Jud Scott at this residence who is a naval officer?"

I replied: "Yes" (wondering who this person might be?)

Then she said:"Does he have a wife named, Ildiko?"

I said:"Yes" again.

After a brief pause she asked: "Did she have a best friend named, Bea?"

My heart was in my throat as I switched to Hungarian and I asked her:" Am I talking to her?"

It was a very special moment for both of us as we talked for a couple of hours sharing lots of laughter and tears trying to catch up with our lives for the last twenty years.

She and her husband have been living in New Mexico for over twenty years now and we made a promise to keep in touch on a regular basis. It has been such a blessing to have her back in my life.

I hope the story of my life will inspire our family, and its later generations, to find a true appreciation for our great country, and always to be thankful for having been born in America. Their father, my husband, Jud, served this country with great honor, as did his father and grandfather. He is so very proud of America's contribution to the world, and so am I. And now our son Nathan continues this great tradition, the fourth consecutive generation of our family to serve as a naval officer. We have a remarkable, exceptional country, and it needs the contributions of all of us to remain great and to grow to further greatness.

I'm also very proud of the majority of the immigrants who left their homeland (and often their families) behind to give their all, and their devotion to this country. They became productive citizens and helped make America the most desirable place to live on this Earth.

For me personally, there are not enough words in the English language to express my gratitude for the many opportunities America has provided me. God brought me through many obstacles that would have stopped me without his intervention. God, America, and my family have given me a life here and a future beyond my wildest childhood dreams.

The Wailing Wall where I fulfilled a promise I had made after I learned what a special place it had been for my father.

Our pilgrimage to the Holy Land. Standing outside the old city wall surrounding Jerusalem, with my special friends who shared my faith journey.

Epilogue

There is, of course, so much more to my story than what I have related here, but it is important to me to pass this history on to our children and to share it with the readers of this book. It is my deepest hope that it also will help our children and later generations of our family find the strength to overcome whatever challenges they may face when Jud and I are no longer here for them in person.

I do believe that both of our children know there is no greater love on Earth than the unconditional love of God, and that we truly honor Him through our unconditional love for family. This is the same powerful love that sustained my father through immense hardship and gave me the strength to believe in my future when things were so bleak. That same love also brought Jud and me together, and it has been at the core of our marriage. I pray and hope that the legacy of our love will continue to nourish their families and their later generations.

We live in interesting times: the world around us is changing rapidly and becoming smaller as people communicate through the Internet instead of face-to-face. This phenomenon is changing societies all over the world. While this great technology helps the business world to communicate with many people at the same time, it also separates us, and we are beginning to lose the art of personal communication. Family members will text and e-mail each other first before they pick up the phone or take time to visit with one another. Young people chat with each other on their laptops for hours instead of listening to each other's voices. Family dinners and prayers before meals are becoming things of the past.

However, the most important things in life, which have not changed and never will, are the need to be loved and appreciated and the basic human desire to love in return. We all have a tremendous need to belong and to find meaning and purpose for our lives. And above all, we need to have faith in our Creator, knowing that without His guidance our lives would be very empty. I can honestly say that without my faith in God and His guidance I could not have survived. There were so many little miracles that helped me survive the chaos of my childhood and come to America. Then, when I thought I was not going to be able to assimilate and make it in this great country, God brought people into my life to help me along and to be there for me during the most difficult and lonely times. Once I discovered and began to understand what makes America the greatest country on Earth, when I understood the opportunities and freedoms available to me to become anything I wanted to be, and when I saw my father's great success though hard work and determination, I myself began to thrive and found my way to become successful.

I learned even more about America when I married my husband. He loves this country with a deep passion and pride and guided me to become involved and try to make a difference whenever I could. I was terribly shy at first and never thought that one person could make a difference. His response was always the same: "Always stand up for what you believe in, pray about it, and just do what you can. It is far better than doing nothing."

I try to follow his lead and stay involved in our community at many levels to make whatever difference I can. It is my way of thanking America for the gift of my life here and the blessing this nation continues to be for millions of immigrants who come here in search of a better life.

My wonderful high school English teacher, Mr. McKown, would be proud of me today. He told me many years ago, "Ildiko, the day you start liking America, she will like you back." My reply to him today would be, "Well, Mr. McKown, I don't just like America; I love her and I will be forever be grateful for the opportunities and for my life here. And thank you, Mr. McKown, for being there for me and for being my first American friend and mentor."

My life today is fuller than ever. I retired from my beloved Nordstrom this year, but the friends I made during my almost thirty years there continue to be a very important part of my life. As I write this, our first grandson is about to be born, and I hope I will be as good a grandmother as the one I had so she can watch me from heaven and be proud of me. I am planning on going back to Hungary this coming year with my best friend, Bea, so we can walk down memory lane and visit every one of those places that hold so many special memories for us both. We will start at the Jewish orphanage where our lifelong friendship began.

My husband, Jud, is going to retire from the court this year also, and we are planning to travel, maybe do some mission work and make many happy memories with our children and grandchildren for as long as we are on this earth. We will cherish our friends, continue to help in our communities, and always do what we can while keeping our eyes on the Lord.

It is truly a joy to watch our children as they are making their mark in this world. Since they are both married now and have started their own families, they will be building their own legacies, which all began so long ago in another time and place.

I would like to express my deepest gratitude again to my family and our many friends who encouraged me for many years to write this story. I hope it has inspired you, the reader, never to give up hope, to sustain an unwavering faith in God, and never to forget or underestimate the power of love and your own human potential. With your own hope and determination, and with God's rich blessings, you, too, have the capacity to thrive, no matter your beginnings or whatever obstacles may confront you.

Acknowledgments

The first person I need thank is my wonderful English teacher, Mr. Harry Mc Mckown. I spent so many Monday nights with him and his wife during my junior and senior year in high school learning the English language, while he got to learn about my life growing up in Hungary. He encouraged me to write my story. His exact words were: " Ildiko, one day when you have mastered the English language, you will need to tell your story; people will read it."

Over the past four decades I lost count of the number of people who asked me to write a story of my life, including many clients, colleagues, close friends and my family. The final decision was made when my children talked to me one day, several years ago, saying: "Mom you have a story to tell and we are the products of your history. You need to write this down so we can have it to tell our children one day." Likewise, for many years my husband also asked me to start writing a book. Eventually I promised my family that I would write my story, and after many years of prayer and thinking, I started the process—that was a little over four years ago.

Thank you, Steve Wagner, for your able assistance; for all the research you did, and for organizing all of the chapters to make it easy for the reader to understand and follow my story.

I would like to thank Alex Johnson for designing the book cover and layout, and the rest of the staff at Alive Book Publishing who have been incredibly supportive and encouraging, for making this book a reality.

Last but not least, I thank my dear friend, Mary Harkin, for referring me to Alive Book Publishing.

I did almost all my writing in Princeville, Kauai at the Cliff Club, overlooking the Pacific Ocean and the majestic Bali Hai. I am grateful for this magical place where I could shut out the world around me and go back in time to where I came from.

I hope you that while you read my story you will take this journey with me.

—Ildiko Scott

ABOOKS

ALIVE Book Publishing and ALIVE Publishing Group
are imprints of Advanced Publishing LLC,
3200 A Danville Blvd., Suite 204, Alamo, California 94507

Telephone: 925.837.7303 Fax: 925.837.6951
www.alivebookpublishing.com

CPSIA information can be obtained at www.ICGtesting.com
Printed in the USA
BVOW08*1123230316

441460BV00003B/5/P

9 781631 320262